THE EXPLAINER

THE EXPLAINER

THE WRITERS AT SLATE MAGAZINE

EDITED BY BRYAN CURTIS · INTRODUCTION BY MICHAEL KINSLEY

ANCHOR BOOKS
A Division of Random House, Inc.
New York

AN ANCHOR BOOKS ORIGINAL, MARCH 2004

Copyright © 2004 by Slate Magazine
Illustrations copyright © 2004 by Mark Matcho

All essays that appear in this book originally appeared on Slate.com.

Library of Congress Cataloging-in-Publication Data
The explainer / the writers at Slate magazine ; edited by Bryan Curtis ;
  introduction by Michael Kinsley.
     p.   cm.
  From the Explainer column of the online magazine Slate.
  ISBN 1-4000-3426-4 (pbk.)
    1. Questions and answers.   I. Curtis, Bryan.
    II. Slate (Redmond, Wash.)
  AG195.E96 2004
    031.02—dc22   2003061831

Book design by Debbie Glasserman

www.anchorbooks.com

Printed in the United States of America
10   9   8   7   6   5   4   3   2   1

CONTENTS

INTRODUCTION: WHAT IS AN EXPLAINER?

The White House correspondent of *The New Republic* in the 1960s and 1970s was an old shoe-leather reporter named John Osborne. A courtly, crusty, southern chain-smoker, he was very much self-styled and quite set in his ways. One of his ways was dictating his stories by telephone if he had the slightest reason to be away from the office. Part of my job in the august role of editor of *The New Republic* was to work the typewriter on the receiving end. John rigorously followed some ancient, real or imagined wire-service ritual of spelling out certain words. "President Carter's national security advisor, Zbigniew Brzezinski," he would intone, adding helpfully, "That's a-d-v-i-s-o-r."

In that spirit, we offer this collection from *Slate*'s popular Explainer column. The idea is this: You're reading the morning paper or listening to the TV news and a question arises in your mind. Despite the best efforts of top journalists, there's something you don't get. Every workday morning, *Slate*'s editors and writers exchange their "I don't get its" by e-mail. Whoever is writing that day's Explainer column then goes off to find the explanation and post it for readers by the afternoon.

As with *Slate*'s other attempts at what we pretentiously call intelligent synthesis, we try to produce Explainers that our readers can use in two different ways. They can treat the column as an introduction and framework for learning more about the subject. Internet hyperlinks are invaluable for this. Or they can use it as an executive briefing, a way to avoid learning any more about the subject. Our goal is to give you exactly enough understanding to bluff your way through the next business meeting or dinner party—but not one bit more than necessary.

Slate's Explainers come in several varieties, correlating with the different ways other media fall down on the explanatory job. (Nothing in *Slate* itself, of course, ever requires further explanation. . . .) Sometimes the dynamics of how a story got into the papers and where its information came from are an important part of the story itself, but dainty journalistic conventions prevent your newspaper from making any of this clear. *The New York Times* might find half a dozen occasions on a typical day to inform its readers that the secretary of state is named Colin Powell. But the *Times* will not tell us whether that "senior American official" they are quoting is also named Powell, and why he is saying such terrible things, off the record, about some other senior official. A daily Explainer might tear off the veil and describe what's really going on. Or it might discard the innards of the news story and explain the journalistic rules about unnamed sources.

Often, especially on TV, there just isn't room for enough background information—even for the dinner-party minimalist—on why two countries are at war or where some singer fits in the pantheon of rock music, or how double-entry bookkeeping differs from keeping two sets of books. Sometimes the problem isn't space but the understandably skewed perceptions of a writer who has been covering NATO for so long that he's forgotten that everyone else has forgotten why or even whether France is a member.

And sometimes there's a question on the minds of 99 percent of those who are following the news on a particular day, but which the other media are too dignified to answer. But very little is beneath the dignity of *Slate,* if sacrificing our dignity will sate the legitimate—or at least understandable—curiosity of our readers. Who are all these people in the news with the same last name, or even first name? Does that presidential proclamation about the need for more tax cuts rhyme on purpose?

The American educated class is plagued by a snobbery you might call knowingness. We don't like to admit, even to ourselves, that we often don't know what the hell others among us are talking about. Print magazines that deal with politics, policy, and culture both high and low often pander to the vanity of knowingness by assuming that their readers already know all about the place of Berlioz in the hierarchy of Romantic music, the philosophical difference between the Constitution and the Articles of Confederation, the names of the last five editors of *Vogue* and why they were fired, who Wendell Willkie was, what the genome is and why it is called that, and so on. As enablers, these publications make the symptoms worse in two ways. First, they flatter their readers with the assumption that they're this knowledgeable. Second, they terrify those same readers by making them worry that everybody else actually does know all this stuff.

From the beginning at *Slate* we have tried to avoid the snobbery of knowingness. We assume that our readers are intelligent and intellectually curious. But we also assume that no one can simultaneously be an expert, or even a well-informed layperson, in all the different areas we write about. (Certainly the founding editor was not, and he was very careful to hire staff members—some of whom are now running the joint—who would not be likely to hurt his feelings with their wide expertise either.) We try to supply context and explanation in everything we publish, but Explainer is where we supply it straight and pure. I'd like to say we do this because our readers are more into intellectual honesty than into petty snobbery about what they may not know. Some of them are, no doubt. For the rest, we help you bluff.

Explainer, by the way, is an old newspaper term for—well, for an article that supplies explanation or exegesis. That's s-u-p-p-l-i-e-s.

—*Michael Kinsley*

THE EXPLAINER

BAD IDEAS

CAN YOU
BREAK EVEN
PLAYING SLOTS?

DOES
**CORKING A
BASEBALL BAT**
HELP A HITTER?

WHAT IF YOU
SKIP
THE CENSUS?

CAN
ICE CUBES
COOL YOUR POOL?

COULD YOU REALLY EARN
**$100
MILLION**
BY TAKING A WIFE?

CAN YOU GIVE YOUR
CONGRESSMAN
HOCKEY TICKETS?

CAN YOU BREAK EVEN PLAYING SLOTS?

Conservative moralist William Bennett claimed he'd "come out pretty close to even" gambling over the past decade, contradicting a report that pegs his losses at around $8 million. Given Bennett's stated preference for high-stakes slot machines and video poker, does his claim hold mathematical water?

As a few lucky Powerball winners can attest, nothing's impossible when it comes to fighting astronomical odds. But it's highly improbable that Bennett has broken even through the years. The primary factor working against the former White House drug czar is his choice of games. Professional gamblers and mathematicians alike eschew slot machines as suckers' bets; since no skill is involved, they're fixed to favor the house, and the rapid action translates into rapid losses. The notion of any machine being hot or cold on a given evening is pure myth, since they're powered by computer chips that function as random number generators. The belief among slot pullers that past losses mean soon-to-be-realized jackpots—the "I'm due" mentality—is referred to as the gambler's fallacy. One bet has absolutely nothing to do with the next.

Slots are fixed to pay out a certain percentage of the money wagered in each machine. In Atlantic City, for example, where Bennett has done much of his gambling, state law sets a minimum payout of 83 percent. However, because of market competition—everyone wants the "Loosest Slots in Town!" title—the actual average is much higher, usually estimated in the range of 90 to 95 percent. (Predictably, casinos are rather cagey about their gaming statistics.) The remaining 5 to 10 percent is referred to as the casino's hold, or take. The high-stakes machines, which Bennett favors, have higher payout percentages, sometimes hitting 98 percent.

Over the long run, of course, the house always wins, thanks to a mathematical principle known as the law of large numbers.

Simply put, the larger the number of plays, the more likely that the fixed probability will catch up with the player. Bennett may have had a lucky night here or there, but after untold thousands of spins, the fixed nature of the slots likely caught up with him: Bennett almost certainly lost between 2 and 10 percent of the millions he bet.

Bennett might have helped his case by following intelligent slots protocol, such as carefully reading the payout rules on each machine (identical-looking slots may feature different maximum payouts, a classic casino trick) and always betting the maximum allowable (which increases the probability of hitting the top jackpot). Over a decade's worth of gaming, however, that's not enough to beat the law.

The wild card (pun intended) in Bennett's hobby was his taste for video poker, which requires a bit of skill rather than just leverpulling. (Gaming experts always recommend video poker over slots.) There are even video poker machines with theoretical long-term payouts exceeding 100 percent—assuming that the player executes a perfect strategy on each and every hand. Since that's not likely, a competent player can expect an average payout ranging from 90 to 98 percent, depending on his skill and the type of machine. Which means he or she is still going to lose in the long run.

WHAT IF YOU SKIP THE CENSUS?

Every year, American households receive census forms sent out by the federal government. Each envelope says, "Your response is required by law." What law is this? Has anybody been prosecuted for not responding?

The Census Bureau likes to stress the positive benefits of participation in the survey, but the proverbial stick does exist. Under federal law, you can be fined up to $100 for refusing to complete a census form and $500 for answering questions falsely. Noncompliance used to bring the possibility of a sixty-day prison sentence and a one-year prison term for false answers, but Congress struck those provisions in 1976.

Although prosecutions are uncommon, people have been successfully tried and convicted. In 1960, for instance, William Rickenbacker of Briarcliff Manor, New York, answered the basic census questions but refused to answer the expanded questionnaire, which asked about the economic status of his household. He argued that it represented an invasion of his privacy. A federal judge disagreed, fining him $100 and handing him a sixty-day suspended prison sentence.

Rickenbacker answered some questions, so his noncompliance was obvious—but how would the federal authorities know about someone who simply refused to return the form? When a census form is not returned, the Census Bureau sends workers to follow up in person. They will return as many as six times to the same residence. That information can be referred to the Justice Department as the basis for prosecution.

Not all prosecutions go smoothly for the government, however. Hawaii resident William Steele appealed a conviction and an accompanying $50 fine he received for not fully answering his questionnaire during the 1970 census. Steele argued that he had been singled out for prosecution because he participated in a public protest against the census. An appeals court agreed and threw out his conviction.

CAN ICE CUBES COOL YOUR POOL?

"Dedicated pool owners are dropping hundreds of pounds of ice into their 90-degree pools in hopes of some relief," The Wall Street Journal *reported in August 1999. "Only one problem: It doesn't really work." Why not? Assume a 15-by-30-foot pool, 6 feet deep. The water is 90 degrees Fahrenheit and you'd like to cool it to 80 degrees. How much ice would that take?*

The pool holds just more than 20,000 gallons of water, all of which is 10 degrees too hot. To raise the temperature of a gallon of water by 1 degree Fahrenheit requires 2,100 calories. To cool a gallon by 1 degree requires getting rid of the same amount. To cool 20,000 gallons by 10 degrees means getting rid of 420,000,000 calories.

Ice cools by absorbing heat in two steps. First it melts; then the resulting water rises to the temperature of its surroundings. It takes about 36,000 calories to melt a pound of ice into 32-degree water. Each pound of ice produces about 0.12 gallons of water. Since it takes 2,100 calories to raise a gallon of water a degree, 0.12 gallons of water will absorb about 12,000 calories in the process of warming from 32 degrees to 80 degrees ([.12 x 2,100] x 48). Taking both steps together, one pound of ice will absorb about 48,000 calories in the process of becoming 80-degree pool water (36,000 to melt and 12,000 to warm).

So to lower the temperature of a 20,000-gallon pool of 90-degree water by 10 degrees, you would need about 8,750 pounds of ice. A 10-pound bag of ice costs around a buck, so cooling your pool with ice cubes would cost $875. (It would also add about 3 inches to the depth of the water.) And, of course, as long as the air around the pool and the bodies in it are warmer than 80 degrees, the water would immediately start getting warmer again.

For those pool owners who would like to personalize this calculation, here's how: (1) Take your pool's volume, in gallons. (2) Divide by 1,000. (3) Multiply by the number of degrees (Fahrenheit) you'd like to cool the water. (4) Multiply that number by 43.75. (5) Think again.

DOES CORKING A BASEBALL BAT HELP A HITTER?

In June 2003, Chicago Cubs slugger Sammy Sosa found himself in hot water for using a corked bat in a game against Tampa Bay. How does corking a bat help a hitter?

Corking a bat lightens the lumber, which in turn increases bat speed and, the conventional wisdom holds, hit distance. Corkers typically drill a hole at the end of the bat, hollow out the sweet spot, and fill it with wine corks or Superballs. The hole is then sealed with a combination of sawdust and pine tar. The result is a bat that's several ounces lighter than advertised, though still as long and thick as its heavier peers. A lighter bat, of course, is easier to whip through the strike zone. The theoretical edge seems infinitesimal. Assume a corker reduces his bat's weight by 1.5 ounces. An average major league pitch travels from the pitcher's hand to the plate in a hair under half a second. The corked bat will give the hitter an additional five-thousandths of a second to see the pitch, judge it, and get the bat head moving through the strike zone.

A quicker bat may help a struggling hitter catch up with pitches, but it actually reduces his ability to smack long drives. The primary equation that determines a batted ball's distance is $p = mv$, where p is momentum, m is mass, and v is velocity. Though a corked bat will travel at a greater velocity, the tail-off in weight lessens the mass. As a result, sluggers like Sosa will actually see the length of their moon shots decrease. In his book *The Physics of Baseball,* Yale physicist Robert K. Adair estimated that a corked bat will shave about a yard off a 400-foot tater.

More likely to benefit, then, are slap hitters who specialize in singles. But the advantage is more psychological than anything else—a corked bat is essentially a placebo for hitters on the skids. They also splinter more readily, which makes catching the cheaters a lot easier. Rather than risk long suspensions, Adair advises, players should opt for lighter bats, perhaps those made of a lighter grain of wood. Or they can just choke up three-quarters of an inch, which produces the same uptick in bat speed as corking.

Bonus Explainer: Surprisingly, the same major league baseball rules that outlaw corking make no mention of minimum or maximum bat weights, although there's a maximum length of 42 inches and a maximum diameter of 2.75 inches. The earliest set of codified rules for professionals, published in 1857, recommended bats that weighed up to 48 ounces. Today, given the abundance of pitchers who throw 95 mph cheese, players prefer much lighter bats; the current average weight is about 33 ounces.

CAN YOU GIVE YOUR CONGRESSMAN HOCKEY TICKETS?

President Clinton spent August 1998 on Martha's Vineyard as the houseguest of a wealthy Bostonian. Renting a comparable house for three weeks would have cost an estimated $10,000 to $15,000, but the president paid nothing. On the other hand, a Federal Trade Commission attorney or a House member, for example, cannot accept even a hockey ticket from a lobbyist. Why the difference? And who decides who can get what?

There are actually four bodies that set ethical standards for federal employees. Representatives are regulated by a House committee, senators by a Senate committee, executive employees (including the president) by congressional statute, and the judiciary by itself. The four sets of rules about gifts vary a little, but all share the common objective of discouraging bribes. (As part of the Republican revolution, both the House and Senate voted themselves stricter rules in 1995, bringing their regulations in line with those they'd imposed on executive employees.)

The rules are: (1) judges and their staffs may not accept gifts; (2) members of the House and their staffs may not accept gifts; (3) executive branch employees—other than the president and vice president—may accept gifts worth less than $20, and no more than $50 worth of gifts from any one source in a year; and (4) senators and their staffs may accept gifts worth less than $50 (one source may give only $100 worth in one year). There are naturally many exceptions and fudges, which differ slightly among the four codes. Friends and family may give unlimited gifts. Trophies, commendations, work-related travel, award money, official dinners, baseball caps, soda pop, coffee, and T-shirts are generally okay. (The House once posted a memo on gift-giving chockfull of real-world examples such as "Laura Lobbyist offers Stanley Staffer tickets to a hockey game taking place in January 1996. Stanley may not accept.")

The most interesting exception to the federal regulations for executive employees applies to exactly two people—the president and the vice president—who are exempted from the limits on gift value. Federal regulations justify the exception "because of considerations relating to the conduct of their offices, including those of protocol and etiquette." The president and vice president may accept gifts of any value from American citizens so long as they don't solicit the gift and aren't influenced by it. A gift from a foreign citizen or government worth less than $245 is acceptable; gifts worth more belong to the U.S. government. When the president accepts certain kinds of gifts from American citizens worth more than $250, he must disclose this fact. In the case of the Vineyard house, though, because it falls into the category of personal hospitality, the president didn't need to reveal the value of this gift on his personal disclosure forms.

COULD YOU REALLY EARN $100 MILLION BY TAKING A WIFE?

In the movie The Bachelor, *a character leaves his grandson $100 million in his will. The catch: To receive his inheritance, the grand-*

son must be married before his thirtieth birthday. Is this sort of restriction legal? And are there any limits on the conditions one can place on a gift?

Grandpa is well within his rights; conditional gifts to people and institutions are not uncommon. Although the laws vary from state to state, judges have generally reasoned that since the beneficiary is free to decline the gift, such conditions don't violate anyone's rights. So wealthy parents are free to put virtually any restriction on their estates. Inherited money is most frequently contingent upon the recipient's getting a college education or staying out of legal trouble. But courts have even upheld parents' right to condition gifts on the heir's abstaining from smoking or marrying someone of a certain religion or ethnicity. And conditional gifts to charities—such as the donation of a university building with the restriction that alcohol not be served on the premises—have long been made. The courts have made only a few exceptions:

1. The condition cannot require a violation of the law. This principle has been used most frequently to prevent beneficiaries from having to uphold illegal racial restrictions in order to receive property. For instance, courts have overturned the proviso that donated parkland be available only to white people.

2. The condition cannot run counter to public policy. Courts vary in their interpretation of this principle but have generally used it to strike down requirements that prohibit marriage or encourage divorce. (Most commonly, a man will attempt to leave property to his wife as long as she never remarries.) It has also been used to repeal requirements that would cause family strife—for example, the provision that inherited land can be used by only one side of the family. And it has prevented beneficiaries from being required to change their religion or name.

3. The condition cannot last forever. Courts consider it undesirable for someone to control property or land for hundreds of years after his death. So in most states, restrictions on private inheritances are limited to the lifetime of living beneficiaries plus twenty-one years (though conditions on bequests to charities can often last longer). After this time, the property and decision rights must be transferred to an individual or a group.

THE CRIMINAL MIND

WHY STEAL **FAMOUS** PAINTINGS?

WHAT'S THE DIFFERENCE **BETWEEN A SPREE KILLER** AND A **SERIAL KILLER?**

HOW OFTEN DO **PRISONERS** ESCAPE?

WHAT IS **NARCISSISTIC** PERSONALITY DISORDER?

INMATES CAN'T VOTE. SO WHY CAN THEY **RUN FOR CONGRESS?**

WHAT IS **MONEY** LAUNDERING?

WHY STEAL FAMOUS PAINTINGS?

In 1998 thieves stole two Van Goghs and one Cézanne from a Rome museum. Police recovered the paintings from the thieves' apartments a few months later. But why steal famous paintings in the first place? They may be worth millions, but how can a thief turn them into cash?

One way is to sell to private buyers. Of course, these buyers cannot display or resell the painting; they are true aesthetes, willing to buy art just to look at it. Sometimes a collector will even commission a criminal to steal a particular work of art. (This is what Italian police initially suspected, since by stealing the Van Goghs and the Cézanne, the bandits passed up several more valuable pieces.) A second way is to extract a ransom from the owner or the insurer of the art. Third, if the painting isn't really famous, the thief can raise money by offering the stolen canvas as collateral for a loan. Even reputable banks don't always check the provenance (record of ownership) of items they take as collateral.

Finally, drug traffickers and other shady characters may use paintings as a sort of international currency that is easy to transport and hard to counterfeit.

WHAT IS NARCISSISTIC PERSONALITY DISORDER?

A 2003 Associated Press story noted that Christian Longo, who killed his wife and three children in 2001, claimed to suffer from narcissistic personality disorder (NPD) during his sentencing hearing. What is NPD, and is it an effective criminal defense?

As the disorder's name suggests, an NPD sufferer believes he or she is the greatest thing since sliced bread. The *Diagnostic and*

Statistical Manual of Mental Disorders lists nine telltale signs, including unrealistic fantasies of living a more glamorous life, a desperate craving for admiration, and a complete lack of empathy for others. Psychiatrists believe that these tendencies are often rooted in childhood insecurity.

Whatever the cause may be, people with NPD basically can't help acting like selfish jerks. They lie incessantly about their accomplishments, treat friends and family like peons, and feel entitled to jet-set lifestyles regardless of their true talents, wealth, or education. There are about 1 million Americans whose self-centeredness is severe enough to merit a diagnosis of NPD; the condition is often exacerbated by depression, substance abuse, or other coexistent mental maladies, such as paranoid personality disorder or borderline personality disorder.

The most severe cases of NPD can lead to violence, especially when the sufferer is rejected or feels his or her fantasy life is threatened. Prosecutors argued, for example, that Longo killed his family because he felt they were an impediment to the life of privilege that he believed he deserved. People with NPD also tend to be excessively impulsive and less able to consider how their actions might affect others.

That doesn't mean, however, that NPD is necessarily a useful defense. When it is mentioned in the courtroom, it's often during the penalty phase, as in Longo's case. The defense hope is that the psychiatric evidence will mitigate the crime's circumstances and thus convince a judge to impose a more lenient sentence. There are no national statistics that track the effectiveness of this strategy, though anecdotal evidence suggests that NPD rarely, if ever, leads to a reduction in sentence. NPD certainly didn't help mitigate Longo's punishment; he was condemned to die. Nor have lawyers had much luck in using NPD alone to build insanity defenses. Even hard-core narcissists know the difference between right and wrong and are in touch with reality. In 2002, for example, a South Dakota man named Kenneth Leon Martin was tried for killing an off-duty police officer. Defense lawyers argued that Martin's NPD led him to fantasize that—like a super-powerful version of the faith healers he'd seen on television—he could raise his victim from the dead. But Martin was convicted;

the jury was convinced by a prosecution psychiatrist that the murderer, despite his disorder, was well aware that shooting an unarmed man was wrong.

WHAT'S THE DIFFERENCE BETWEEN A SPREE KILLER AND A SERIAL KILLER?

The snipers who terrorized the Washington, D.C. area in 2002 were alternately referred to in the press as serial killers and spree killers. What's the difference?

The classic serial killer takes breaks between slayings, ranging from weeks to months. Victims usually fit a particular profile, such as prostitutes or elderly women; the former are a favorite target, as their disappearances seldom provoke much alarm from police. Serial killer Jeffrey Dahmer, for example, preyed chiefly upon gay hustlers, a community that existed on Milwaukee's fringes. Sex somehow plays into the bulk of serial killings. Victims are often molested, or selected because they strike a dark Freudian chord with the murderer.

Spree killers, on the other hand, pack their mayhem into a brief time span; killing becomes a full-time job, so to speak. The spree is often precipitated by a specific rage-inducing event, such as a romantic breakup or family spat. Loved ones are typically the initial victims; the killer then goes on the lam, slaughtering people along the way without much forethought. These victims do not fit any discernible profile but may be dispatched out of necessity—say, because the killer needs their car. Because of the high-profile, indiscriminate nature of the killings, police attention is intense, and the killer is usually apprehended (or commits suicide) after a few weeks. Andrew Cunanan, who chalked up five murders during a 1997 cross-country trek, is often pointed to as the prototypical spree killer.

The Washington sniper suspects didn't quite conform to this taxonomy of evil. The frequency of the killings and randomness of the victims suggested they were standard spree killers. But they allegedly confined their activity to one geographic area and premeditated the slayings, two peculiarities that jibe more closely with the model of a serial killer.

HOW OFTEN DO PRISONERS ESCAPE?

Six escaped convicts from an Alabama prison were arrested in January 2001, the same month the last two of the infamous Texas Seven fugitives surrendered in Colorado. How often do American prisoners escape?

Not very. In 1998, the most recent year for which data were available from the Bureau of Justice Statistics, 6,530 people escaped or went AWOL from state prisons. That was a little more than half of 1 percent of the total population of 1,100,224 state prisoners.

And the numbers are declining. Fewer people have escaped from state prisons every year since 1994, and the percentage of prisoners escaping or going AWOL has fallen steadily, too. In 1993, 14,305 prisoners escaped out of a prison population of 780,357. That's almost 2 percent.

True, there are still thousands of escapees a year. Why aren't you hearing about them? The vast majority of escapees are "walkaways" from community corrections facilities that have minimal supervision. Dramatic Hollywood-style escapes from maximum security prisons are the ones that draw media attention.

Like their maximum security counterparts, the minimum security walkaways are usually recovered. State prisons reported that more escapees and AWOL prisoners were returned than escaped every year from 1995 to 1998. Breakouts from federal prisons are rarer than escapes from state prisons. One federal prisoner escaped and was recaptured in 1999, out of a prison population of more than 115,000.

WHAT IS MONEY LAUNDERING?

In September 1999, federal investigators suspected that Russian mobsters may have used the Bank of New York to launder as much as $10 billion. What is money laundering and how does it work?

In short, money laundering is the conversion of illegally obtained profits into funds that appear legitimate—that is, making dirty money clean. It is used by drug traffickers, arms smugglers, and anyone else who needs to spend ill-gotten gains without arousing suspicion. White-collar criminals and corrupt political leaders also frequently launder funds to avoid taxes or conceal embezzlement.

The simplest form of money laundering is combining criminal profits with earnings from a legitimate cash-intensive business. For example, say a drug dealer wants to disguise $10,000 in monthly profits from cocaine sales. So he buys a bar that takes in $50,000 a month—mostly in cash. At the end of each month, he slips an extra $10,000 into his till and reports $60,000 in bar revenue. Although his drug income is now taxable, it is worth that price to make the profits appear legal.

Larger amounts—say, $10 billion—can't just be slipped into the till. Laundering big sums generally involves three steps:

Placement: The cash proceeds (often thousands of bills in small denominations) enter the legitimate banking system. Many countries require that large cash transactions (in the United States, anything above $10,000) be reported to authorities. So launderers often deposit proceeds piece by piece or export the money to countries with relaxed banking regulations.

Layering: The money is separated from its criminal origins through complex financial transactions. Often, funds will be transferred dozens of times through multiple accounts, companies, and countries, making the paper trail virtually impossible to follow.

Integration: The money returns to its original source, apparently as legitimate income.

There are countless variations on this pattern. One of the most common is the loan-back scheme, in which the launderer essentially borrows money from himself. First, he sets up a lending company in a country with few financial regulations. Then he fills its coffers with illegal profits, layered through multiple accounts. When the launderer wants to make a purchase in his home country, he simply "borrows" the money from the overseas lender. This money, once illegal, now appears to be a legitimate loan.

INMATES CAN'T VOTE. SO WHY CAN THEY RUN FOR CONGRESS?

When former representative James Traficant was carted off to jail after his conviction on multiple felonies, he told the judge that he expected to be reelected from his jail cell. As an inmate, the former Ohio rep was in a strange position—free to run for federal office, but prohibited from voting. Why do states let inmates run but not vote?

In fact, every state in the Union allows its inmates to run but not vote, except for Maine and Vermont, which allow them to do both. This strange setup exists because Supreme Court precedent says states can't prohibit inmates from running but can disenfranchise them.

In a 1974 case, *Richardson v. Ramirez,* the Supreme Court upheld a California law disenfranchising felons. The court based its argument on Section 2 of the Fourteenth Amendment, which was supposed to create an incentive for southern states to let blacks vote. The amendment reduced the number of representatives allotted to states that denied the vote to any male inhabitants "except for participation in rebellion, or other crime"—a phrase that the majority found to justify disenfranchising felons.

A ruling in a 1995 term limits case, *U.S. Term Limits, Inc. v. Thornton,* gave inmates the freedom to run for Congress. The Supreme Court invalidated an Arkansas term limits amendment, arguing that the qualifications for membership in Congress listed

in Article I of the Constitution were intended to be the full qualifications, and neither Congress itself nor the states can fiddle
with them. Justice Clarence Thomas noted in his dissent that the
majority's ruling meant that states couldn't disqualify prisoners
from running.

One argument for the current setup: Taking away the right to
vote punishes only the inmate, whereas if we want him in office,
taking away his right to run punishes all of us.

DEATH

WHY DO THE **JAPANESE** COMMIT **HARA-KIRI?**

DOES **HOMEOWNER'S INSURANCE** COVER **MURDER?**

HOW DO WE KNOW THAT **1,100 WORLD WAR II VETS DIE EVERY DAY?**

WHEN DOES THE **FLAG FLY AT HALF-STAFF?**

WHAT'S WITH THE **BRIGHT LIGHTS** YOU SEE BEFORE YOU DIE?

ARE **DEAD BODIES** DANGEROUS?

DOES HOMEOWNER'S INSURANCE COVER MURDER?

The parents of the perpetrators of the Columbine school shooting agreed to pay the families of some of the victims $1.6 million in settled lawsuits. The money was to come from the parents' homeowner's insurance. How is it that a homeowner's policy covers murder?

Besides giving you money to rebuild your house if it's struck by lightning or to replace your jewelry if it's stolen by thieves, a homeowner's policy has a liability clause that insures the homeowner against harm caused to others by the homeowner or family members living at the house. But this liability generally covers *accidental* harm, and both of the Columbine killers, Eric Harris and Dylan Klebold, committed premeditated murder. The reason the liability clause covered this settlement is that the lawyers for the victims sued the killers' parents for being negligent in the supervision of their children.

Although homeowner's policies are not required by law, they are required by lenders in order to secure a mortgage, so 96 percent of homeowners have the insurance. (Only 29 percent of renters have insurance that gives similar protection.) People with a lot of assets often get a personal umbrella liability policy, which can add $1 million or more in coverage and provides protection for a larger range of claims such as libel, slander, or mental anguish. Bill Clinton had such a homeowner's umbrella policy and used it to help pay his lawyers' fees and settlement costs in the sexual harassment case brought against him by Paula Jones.

WHY DO THE JAPANESE COMMIT HARA-KIRI?

A former Bridgestone tire executive committed hara-kiri in March 1999 in his boss's Tokyo office. Newspapers tell us that suicide by hara-kiri is rare, but not unheard of, in modern Japan. Why do Japanese commit hara-kiri?

Hara-kiri is a ritualized form of suicide with roots in twelfth-century Japanese samurai warrior culture. Rather than be captured, a defeated swordsman would stab himself in the left belly, draw the blade to the right, then pull upward. *Encyclopaedia Britannica* adds that "it was considered exemplary form to stab again below the chest and press downward across the first cut, and then to pierce one's throat." Obviously, bleeding to death from a gut wound or suffocating from a throat wound is a slow and miserable way to die. As practiced by defeated samurai, it was meant as atonement. It also demonstrated enormous psychological courage, which was a way of winning back some measure of honor even in defeat.

In later years, Japanese officials would sometimes commit hara-kiri to protest a superior's decision. Like self-immolation, hara-kiri is meant to attract attention and show a willingness to sacrifice oneself for a greater cause. Japanese officials sometimes killed themselves to atone for botching an assignment, or out of grief over a leader's death. When the Mejii emperor died in 1912, his leading general committed hara-kiri out of respect for his departed boss.

From at least the fifteenth century, the Japanese emperor employed hara-kiri as a punishment, sending a messenger to give a ceremonial dagger to the person he wanted dead. The unlucky recipient had no choice, of course, but because the death was self-inflicted it was considered more honorable than ordinary execution. Often, in a concession to physical suffering, a friend standing behind him would lop off the condemned man's head just after he stabbed himself. (Novelist Yukio Mishima received such an assist from a colleague when he committed hara-kiri in 1970.) Sometimes, in an even more symbolic version of the ritual, the friend would lop off the condemned man's head as he reached out for the dagger but before he stabbed himself.

Microsoft's *Encarta* encyclopedia says that for many centuries there were an estimated 1,500 instances of voluntary and obligatory hara-kiri per year. But in 1868 or 1873 (sources disagree) the emperor abolished obligatory hara-kiri, and voluntary procedures became less frequent as well. Still, during World War II, many Japanese soldiers committed hara-kiri rather than tolerate capture.

Bonus Explainer: Incidentally, hara-kiri (meaning "belly cutting") is not the word that most Japanese use to describe ritual suicide. The common term for the practice in Japan is seppuku, which roughly translates to "self-disembowelment."

HOW DO WE KNOW THAT 1,100 WORLD WAR II VETS DIE EVERY DAY?

On May 28, 2001, President Bush signed a law for the creation of a monument on the National Mall to honor veterans of World War II. The bill was urgent, he said, because 1,100 of these veterans are dying every day. How do we know how many World War II veterans are dying?

Of course nobody keeps track of how many veterans die every day. The number Bush cited is a statistical estimate calculated each year by the Department of Veterans Affairs based on the age demographics and mortality rates of the greatest generation. The raw data comes from a question on the decennial U.S. census that asks citizens about their military service. Using the most recent census data from 2000, the VA estimates that of the 16.1 million who served in the armed forces during World War II, 4.76 million are alive today—nearly 700,000 fewer than when Bush made his speech. According to these estimates, during the twelve-month period ending September 2003 about 392,000 of them will die, for an average of 1,074 a day. The median age for veterans is 76.7 years and there are over 700 living centenarians. To get a sense of comparison, the National Center for Health Statistics reports that in 1999, 2,391,399 Americans of all ages died, for an average of 6,600 a day. For those older than 70, the annual rate was 1,610,636, or 4,413 a day.

WHEN DOES THE FLAG FLY AT HALF-STAFF?

Flags across the country flew at half-staff as a memorial to those killed in the September 11 terrorist attacks. What are the laws governing the lowering of the flag—and is the proper term half-staff *or* half-mast?

Dictionaries list *half-mast* (the term first appeared in 1627) as the primary entry, but the U.S. government prefers the newer (1708) *half-staff* when referring to the lowering of the flag as a sign of mourning and respect. According to the federal law governing the displaying of the flag, by presidential order the flag is flown at half-staff upon the death of major officials of the federal government or a state governor. The president also has discretionary powers to lower the flag for lower-level officials or foreign dignitaries. The state governors themselves can also order flags to be lowered in their states in honor of the death of current or former officials.

Federal law is quite specific about the length of time the flag should be lowered to honor a deceased officeholder. Presidents or former presidents are granted thirty days at half-staff; the vice president, chief justice of the Supreme Court (current or retired), and speaker of the House get ten. For associate justices to the Supreme Court, cabinet secretaries, former vice presidents, and state governors, the flag should be lowered until their interment. Members of Congress are honored on the day of and the day following their deaths.

While the code is specific about this honor being reserved for government officials, in practice it is used more broadly as a sign of mourning. The method laid out in the law for flying a flag at half-staff is to first raise the flag completely, then lower it to the half-staff position. At the end of the day the flag is again raised briefly before being fully lowered.

ARE DEAD BODIES DANGEROUS?

News reports covering the 1999 earthquake in Turkey emphasized the health dangers posed by the decomposing bodies of its victims. The Turkish government dug mass graves, and Muslim clerics suspended Islamic burial rules so that the country could dispose of corpses more quickly. Do dead bodies endanger public health?

According to the World Health Organization (WHO), the rotting corpses of earthquake victims were a negligible threat to public health.

A corpse is a danger to public health only if the victim died of an infectious disease. (In that case, the disease organisms can infect living people who come in contact with the cadaver.) But when someone dies of trauma, as most earthquake victims did, the decomposition process is harmless, if disgusting. Bacteria within the body—especially *E. coli* from the gut—immediately start to consume the flesh. Maggots hatched from eggs laid in the corpse also eat the cadaver, as can wasps, beetles, and other insects. Larger animals such as birds, rats, and dogs pick at unguarded corpses.

The bacteria involved in decomposition are not dangerous, because living people already carry identical germs in their own bodies. The maggots and other insects, though revolting, also constitute no threat to public health. Rats do host fleas, which can transmit typhus, typhoid fever, the plague, and other diseases. But rats endanger public health wherever they mingle with people: They are no more harmful when they feed on corpses than at any other time. Despite fears of death's "miasma," a belief rooted in ancient times, the foul odor emitted by the body as it rots is innocuous.

Some reports hinted that unburied corpses could contaminate Turkey's water supply. This was not a serious danger. In a very few cases, bacteria from corpses can cause illness when they contaminate drinking water in large quantities. But water in Turkey was much more likely to be contaminated in other ways, especially when sewer lines ruptured, dumping bacteria into reservoirs and aquifers.

Because the public health threat from corpses is minimal, the WHO urged Turkey to allocate more resources to aiding the injured and fewer to disposing of the dead.

WHAT'S WITH THE BRIGHT LIGHTS YOU SEE BEFORE YOU DIE?

In September 2002, a train operator was killed when his vehicle crashed. Before succumbing to his injuries, he told rescue workers: "I can't see you anymore—all I see is a bright light." Why do the mortally wounded often report seeing a bright light before dying?

Assuming it's not the Great Beyond, medical science has advanced several theories as to the bright light's physiological roots. Many researchers ascribe the glow to the effects of anoxia, or oxygen deprivation, which can affect the optic nerves. Others suspect that trauma to the right temporal lobe, the area of the brain responsible for perception, can cause the senses to malfunction. Michael A. Persinger, a neuroscientist at Laurentian University in Sudbury, Ontario, has replicated the bright-light phenomenon in test subjects by stimulating their right temporal lobes with mild electromagnetic fields.

A third theory holds that the brain releases massive amounts of endorphins, or natural painkillers, when the body is gravely injured. Those endorphins may override the optic nerves, causing the victim to see a peaceful glow rather than their own mangled body or teams of desperate paramedics scurrying about. This endorphin-induced serenity can be crucial to warding off lethal shock, thus giving the person better odds of survival.

It has also been suggested that some bright-light glimpsers neither gaze at eternity nor experience unusual neurological activity. Instead, they may simply mistake the high-intensity operating room lights as something a tad more mystical.

Bonus Explainer: In Western societies, the bright light is often accompanied by visions of deceased relatives, idyllic gardens, and a convivial bearded man in flowing white robes—all standard images of the Christian heaven. Dying Hindus in India, by contrast, typically picture the afterlife as a Kafkaesque bureaucratic office. Fading Micronesians have been known to describe a bustling, skyscraper-filled metropolis.

FORCES OF NATURE

HOW DO YOU **STOP** A LAVA FLOW?

WHAT ARE **HEAT KINKS?**

HOW DO YOU **MEASURE** SNOWFALL?

HOW DO YOU **RATE** A FOREST FIRE?

HOW DO YOU **FIGURE** THE ODDS OF AN **ASTEROID** HITTING THE EARTH?

IS THE **RICHTER SCALE** OBSOLETE?

HOW DO YOU STOP A LAVA FLOW?

In October 2002, Sicily's Mount Etna began spewing molten rock, after a series of earthquakes had sparked the volcano's first major eruption since 1992. Is there any way to stop a lava flow?

Not dead in its tracks per se, but there are some viable tricks to slowing down the deadly stream. The Italians' efforts to stymie Etna's lava date back to 1668, when a retaining wall was built on the mountainside. (It didn't work.) They have had more success in recent years, particularly 1983 and 1992, when hastily constructed earthen barriers managed to slow the flows, which typically sluice down Etna at a few dozen meters per hour. The lava eventually breached the barriers, but it was stalled enough to atrophy before it scorched inhabited land.

Some anti-lava types put their stock in explosives. Back in 1935, a young George S. Patton (then a lieutenant colonel) led an aerial bombing strike against Hawaii's Mauna Loa, hoping to divert the lava away from the city of Hilo; this didn't work. But others have had success with dynamiting the narrow lava tubes through which the 1,800-degree rock travels. By widening the tubes, engineers force the lava to lose energy and dissipate higher up on the volcano. The Italians used this technique as well in 1992, with good results.

The most spectacular anti-lava effort in history occurred on the Icelandic island of Heimaey in 1973. Worried that the lava would flow into the harbor's mouth, forever closing the vital port to ships, Icelanders came up with an ingenious plan. They sprayed the flow with 6 million cubic meters of water, hoping to cool the lava enough—by about 50 degrees Celsius—so that it would solidify. It took five months of nearly constant spraying, using pumps and fire hoses, to atrophy the lava, but the scheme succeeded. But most volcano fighters do not have the luxury of such time. When all else fails, there is always the ancient Hawaiian method: sending a holy figure to the edge of the flow to make an appeal to Pele, the volcano goddess. Many Hawaiians credited the prayers of Princess Ruth Keelikolani with stopping an 1881 lava flow that threatened Hilo.

WHAT ARE HEAT KINKS?

Investigators theorized that a July 2002 Amtrak derailment near Washington, D.C. was caused by a heat kink in the track. What's a heat kink?

Think back to an axiom taught in countless elementary school science classes: Metal expands when heated. As temperature increases, metal atoms gain energy and begin to move more briskly. These active atoms require more space and push adjacent atoms farther away. The end result is a chunk of metal that bloats and bends. This is why Mom submerged jars with hard-to-unscrew lids in boiling water: The atoms get energized, the lid expands, and the Miracle Whip suddenly becomes accessible.

Railroad tracks are no different. When air temperatures approach 100 degrees, small patches of track can bow out several inches, sometimes even a foot or more. Sunlight provides the necessary heat, and metal fatigue and design imperfections make the tracks more malleable. Heat kinks—also known as sun kinks or, more formally, thermal misalignments—primarily affect welded tracks, such as the one near Washington, which use continuous bars of metal as a means of reducing noise and enabling great speed. Older, jointed tracks feature small gaps that can accommodate moderate expansion—much like metal bridges, which are typically studded with mesh-covered cracks to prevent buckling in hot weather.

A heat kink does not make a derailment inevitable. Speed, weight, and track curvature combine to determine a train's fate.

Slower choo-choos are less apt to succumb to heat kinks; after a 1998 accident in Texas, Union Pacific Railroad mandated that trains not exceed 10 mph through areas with known or suspected kinks.

That rule wouldn't have helped the ill-fated Amtrak train, since neither inspectors nor other trains had noticed any warping prior to the crash. Kinks can develop in a matter of hours, so even twice-daily visual inspections are sometimes insufficient. One possible solution is fiber-optic cable, which can be affixed to rails and sound an alarm whenever flaws arise. Researchers at the University of Illinois, Urbana-Champaign, began developing such a system in the mid 1990s.

HOW DO YOU MEASURE SNOWFALL?

The blizzard that pounded the East Coast in February 2003 was one of the region's worst in terms of snowfall. Every year, a new blizzard seems to break some record or another. How do meteorologists figure out how much of the white stuff tumbled down?

Science may have unlocked the secrets of the atom and sent probes past Jupiter, but it has yet to devise a foolproof automated means of measuring snowfall. The most reliable technique still involves a human and a special ruler, divided into tenths of an inch. Before a snowfall, an observer typically lays out several snowboards—not of the recreational variety, but rather simple 16-inch-by-16-inch planks, which are marked with bright flags. Ideally, these boards should be located in wide-open areas where drifting will be minimal. The National Weather Service recommends that every six hours the observer plunge his or her ruler into the snow that's accumulated atop the various boards; after a measurement is taken, the board should be dug up and placed on the freshest layer of snow. Average together the measurements taken from a dozen or so boards, and you've got your snowfall estimate.

The ruler method isn't quite perfect. Some snow may melt between measurements, and strong winds can cause excessive drifting or blowing, even in open terrain. Plus, it's often hard to determine whether there's any frozen rain in the mix—the NWS frowns upon adding frozen rain totals to snowfall estimates. Still, trudging out with a ruler is a good deal more accurate than the alternate technique, whereby snow is collected in a cylindrical gauge and then melted. Under this method, the general guideline is that 10 inches of snow is equal to 1 inch of water. This approach is favored for remote spots where observers may not be around to take manual measurements every day; the gauge is simply lined with antifreeze, to hasten melting, and can potentially be monitored from afar.

The problem is that the ratio of 10 to 1 is merely a rough guesstimate. The actual water content varies widely, depending on the character of the snow. For the slushy stuff common to urban areas, the content may be more along the lines of 6 inches of snow per inch of water; the driest powder, by contrast, can pack 50 inches of snow into the same space. Unless you're on the scene during the snowfall, it's virtually impossible to tell exactly what varieties of snow fell during the blizzard, and in what proportions.

HOW DO YOU RATE A FOREST FIRE?

News stories of wildfires invariably report some level of containment reached by firefighters. What does it mean to contain a fire, how is the percentage calculated, and when is a fire controlled?

To prevent a blaze from spreading, firefighters dig a fire line around its circumference. If 3 miles of fire line have been built around a fire that is 10 miles in circumference, then 30 percent of the fire is considered to be contained.

Fire lines are trenches dug to create a fuel break around the fire. Fires need fuel, oxygen, and heat to burn, and the easiest of the three to eliminate is fuel. Fire lines can also include natural barriers such as roads, rock bluffs, or streams.

Once a fire is fully contained, firefighters work on controlling it by battling it inside the containment line. A controlled fire is one that has no risk of expanding beyond the fire line.

HOW DO YOU FIGURE THE ODDS OF AN ASTEROID HITTING THE EARTH?

Scientists gave a newly discovered asteroid, dubbed 2002 NT7, a 1 in 200,000 chance of striking the Earth on February 1, 2019. How did scientists figure out those odds?

The hazards posed by Near-Earth Asteroids are assessed by Sentry, a computer system developed by the Near-Earth Objects Group at NASA's Jet Propulsion Laboratory in Pasadena, California. The software factors together a cosmic rock's coordinates, distance, velocity, and gravitational influences to calculate its trajectory. The asteroid 2002 NT7, for example, rounds the sun once every 837 days, and our fragile planet will almost certainly pass through its orbital path on February 1, 2019. The big question is where the asteroid will be on that potentially fateful date—behind us, beyond us, or smack-dab in the middle of Kansas.

The long odds are figured from the wildly inaccurate data provided to Sentry. It's easy enough to gauge an asteroid's longitude and latitude (ascension and declination, in astro-speak), but figuring out its current celestial position is tricky. The only way to judge distance and velocity is by tracking the object's movement relative to the stars in the background. This painstaking process requires months or years of observation in order to be accurate, which means initial estimates of position are likely to be off by tens of millions of miles. As Sentry is fed additional data, its guess as to an asteroid's speed and location becomes more precise.

For two weeks, 2002 NT7 sat atop JPL's Current Impact Risks chart, which lists the Near-Earth Asteroids most likely to dinosaur the human race. Along with 1997 XR2, it was one of only two asteroids to earn a 1 on the Torino scale, which ranks the likelihood of collision from 1 ("merits careful monitoring") to 10 (cash in your IRA now). If the 2-kilometer-wide 2002 NT7 were to strike, its impact would release 1 million megatons of energy, about the strength of 20,000 H-bombs exploding simultaneously.

IS THE RICHTER SCALE OBSOLETE?

A 2001 Seattle earthquake registered 6.8 on the . . . well, not on the Richter scale, which The New York Times *reported has been displaced. Is the Richter scale obsolete, and what measure is used instead?*

While the Richter scale is not obsolete, the universal measurement today is the moment magnitude scale. The Richter scale was developed by seismologist Charles Richter (1900–1985) in the 1930s to apply consistent, objective criteria in evaluating the size of earthquakes. Using data from seismographs—which measure earth movement—Richter devised a method to calculate where an earthquake began (its epicenter) and its magnitude. The way the scale works, each whole-number increase—say, from 4.8 to 5.8 to 6.8—represents a tenfold increase in the size of the ground motion.

As effective a tool as the Richter scale is, it has some drawbacks. For one, it is a relative measure; that is, it was developed to compare the size of one earthquake to another. But scientists wanted something that measured an earthquake not just in comparative terms, but in absolute terms. They wanted to get a physical snapshot of how much energy was released when a fault slipped. For another, although the Richter scale was revised to be used to measure earthquakes in other parts of the world, it had limitations, since it was based on conditions in California (where Richter himself was based). Scientists wanted a measurement that was universally applicable.

With the creation of more sophisticated seismology equipment in the 1970s, scientists could determine the actual area where the rupture in the fault took place and measure how much energy was released there during the earthquake, a calculation they call the seismic moment. Because the Richter scale had become so commonly understood, they devised a method to convert the information from the seismic moment into a scale comparable to Richter's, or what's now known as the moment magnitude scale. It is also possible to compare earthquakes measured according to the new scale to those measured in the past on the Richter scale. Although the two scales may use different methods, they should end up producing virtually the same number. Many news organizations have dropped the word *Richter* but have not adopted the phrase *moment magnitude*. Instead the common shorthand is to describe an earthquake as being of a magnitude [fill in the number].

FLIGHT

WHAT DO **AUTOPILOTS** DO?

DID WITNESSES **REALLY** HEAR THE **COLUMBIA** SPLIT APART?

WHY ARE WE **STILL** USING SPY PLANES?

WHAT IS THE **COSMIC RADIATION** THAT'S KO'-ING OUR **ASTRONAUTS?**

COULD **EJECTION** SEATS HAVE SAVED **THE COLUMBIA** ASTRONAUTS?

IS THERE **REALLY** SUCH A THING AS A **WATER LANDING?**

WHAT DO AUTOPILOTS DO?

News reports about the 1999 crash of EgyptAir Flight 990 focused on the use of the airplane's autopilot system. What exactly do autopilots do?

The autopilot is an electronic system that manipulates the three control surfaces that determine an airplane's course: the movable panels, called ailerons, on the trailing edge of each wing that allow the plane to bank right or left; the tail rudder, which turns the aircraft's nose; and the elevators, which point the plane up or down. The autothrottle, which determines the airplane's speed, is controlled by a separate system.

On commercial aircraft, the autopilot and autothrottle are controlled by an advanced onboard navigational computer called the flight management system (FMS). Typically, a pilot programs the FMS before takeoff, entering landmarks, altitude, and desired speed; during flight, the FMS uses instrument readings and radio signals from fixed points on the ground to figure out what adjustments are needed to meet the flight plan.

Autopilots have several advantages. Primarily, they help keep the crew from getting tired, leaving them free to alter the flight plan, scout for traffic, and monitor the plane's other systems (such as hydraulics and air pressurization). Autopilots also improve fuel efficiency and passenger comfort, since the adjustments made by an autopilot are more subtle and accurate than those made by hand.

That's why autopilots are typically engaged on commercial aircraft throughout nearly the entire flight. When human pilots take control—usually during takeoff and landing, and occasionally in midflight—it's largely because they need to stay in practice, not because the autopilot would be unable to fly safely. (In fact, in bad weather, the Federal Aviation Administration may require that pilots allow the autopilot and FMS, which don't rely on

visual cues, to land the plane.) Pilots also take command in tur-
bulence, since an autopilot would waste fuel and possibly exacer-
bate the bumps by making many adjustments to keep the plane
on a steady course. If a pilot doesn't disengage the autopilot
before taking control, the FMS interprets his movements as outside forces and instructs the autopilot to work against them.

DID WITNESSES REALLY HEAR THE <u>COLUMBIA</u> SPLIT APART?

*Several witnesses in North Texas claimed to have heard the space
shuttle* Columbia *split apart, despite the fact that the craft was 40
miles above the Earth. Is it really possible to hear catastrophic events
that occur at such a high altitude?*

It's most likely that the Texans mistook an amalgamation of post-
incineration sonic booms for the *Columbia*'s fatal moment. By
now, Sunbelters are used to the thunderous cracks caused by a
shuttle's reentry. As the vehicle crosses from space into the atmosphere, its supersonic descent stirs up shock waves by compress-
ing the surrounding air. The Physics 101 analogy is the way a boat
causes ripples as it moves through the water—the faster and bigger the boat, the more turbulent the ensuing ripples. The space
shuttle is both fast (the *Columbia* was traveling at 18 times the
speed of sound when it broke up) and big (approximately 122 feet
long), so the shock waves it creates are mighty. When they finally
reach a listener's ears, the resulting sound resembles two sharp
booms in sequence: One is caused by the waves emanating from
the shuttle's nose, the other by those shimmying off the tail.

  In the case of the *Columbia,* however, the craft was split into
thousands upon thousands of chunks of debris, each of which
produced a smaller sonic boom of its own. The rapid series of relatively diminutive booms could easily be mistaken for an explosion. Plus, the blastlike sound of the booms may have been
enhanced by an aural effect known as atmospheric scattering,
whereby the shock waves disperse in midair and play tricks on the

observers' ears. People who have heard shuttle-caused sonic booms often speculate that the reverberation is caused by a reflection off mountains or other geographic features; in fact, these effects are merely caused by the spreading out of the waves as they make their way toward the ground.

It is not impossible that some observers heard the actual rending apart of the *Columbia,* but the final verdict on the veracity of their claims will have to wait for the investigation to be completed. If an explosion occurred, the blast would indeed release energy in the form of audible shock waves (although they might be hard to differentiate from the debris-caused booms). On the other hand, if the ill-fated shuttle merely disintegrated, the odds of hearing that event from 40 miles below are rather slim.

WHAT IS THE COSMIC RADIATION THAT'S KO'-ING OUR ASTRONAUTS?

In summer 2002, NASA barred veteran astronaut Donald Thomas from serving on the International Space Station, citing concerns over his long-term exposure to cosmic radiation. What is cosmic radiation?

Perhaps best known as the mysterious force that gave comicdom's Fantastic Four their superpowers, cosmic radiation is omnipresent in the universe. Much of it consists of low-energy subatomic particles left over from the Big Bang's aftermath—a sort of interstellar background noise. These photons and neutrinos are not considered hazardous to humans.

More worrisome is the radiation produced by solar flares, periodic eruptions during which the sun releases energy equivalent to a billion megatons of TNT. The Earth is protected from these lethal streams by the atmosphere and ozone layer, two luxuries not enjoyed by astronauts. If a spacewalker was to be inadvertently exposed to solar flare radiation, odds are that he or she would be struck down by radiation sickness. The good news is that since solar flares can be detected before the particles arrive, there is often plenty of time for a spacewalker to find a well-shielded spot aboard a spacecraft.

But even shielding does little good against so-called galactic cosmic radiation (GCR), which originates in deep space. Consisting chiefly of high-energy protons and electrons produced by stars, black holes, and gamma ray bursts, GCR is tough to defend against. Shields help a little, but they can't stop every subatomic bit. Astronauts who spend too much time aloft are believed to dramatically raise their risk of developing cancer, although they're not in immediate danger of suffering from radiation sickness.

How much time in space is too much? A precise correlation between GCR exposure and cancer has yet to be established, but NASA was worried enough to hold back Thomas, who had spent 43 days in space on four previous missions. The Russians, however, seem a bit more carefree with their spacemen's well-being. Space station resident Nikolai Budarin once spent nearly ten months aboard *Mir*.

Bonus Explainer: NASA's not the only organization to fret over cosmic radiation. The Association of Flight Attendants has voiced similar concerns, arguing that commercial flights are subject to similar hazard. The union cites Federal Aviation Administration figures that estimate that 27,000 hours of flight time—a reasonable amount of time in the career of a flight attendant—can lead to a 1 percent increase in the odds of dying from cancer.

WHY ARE WE STILL USING SPY PLANES?

In January 2003, one of the Air Force's U-2 spy planes crashed into a South Korean car-repair shop, injuring three people on the ground. In the age of satellites, why is the American military still using the 48-year-old U-2 for its aerial surveillance needs?

Today's U-2s are much improved over the version that Francis Gary Powers piloted into infamy in 1960, when he was felled by a Soviet surface-to-air missile. Lockheed has steadily increased the U-2's wingspan, fuel capacity, and engine power, as well as the sensitivity of onboard sensors that detect incoming hazards. The latest crop of U-2s, which were built in the 1980s, are reported to fly well above 70,000 feet, although the exact altitude ceiling is classified. In any event, not a single U-2 has been gunned down in the post–Cold War era.

The U-2 is notoriously difficult to pilot, a fact that has earned it the nickname Dragon Lady; there are only about fifty pilots qualified to handle the craft, not to mention endure ten hours in a fully pressurized flight suit. Yet the U-2 is still a lot more reliable than Lockheed's other celebrated spy plane, the SR-71 Blackbird, which was officially retired in 1993. The Blackbird wowed with its sleek looks and Mach 3 speed, but it was a royal pain to operate. It required extra-long runways for takeoff, leaked fuel on takeoff, and guzzled gas midflight; nearly all Blackbird missions originated from domestic air bases, where the sensitive planes could be lovingly tended. The U-2, by contrast, is a less fickle machine that can be deployed from virtually any runway.

Satellites have often been proposed as an alternative to U-2s, since no enemy projectile can reach into space. But because they're virtual slaves to their orbits, satellites cannot circle over a specific target. And foes with even middling intelligence can usually figure out when American satellites are passing overhead and cease suspicious activity during those times. That's why the military continues to rely heavily on U-2s, particularly in combat situations. A *Defense Week* source estimated that during the first Gulf War, U-2s provided 90 percent of targeting information to American ground forces, and that during the NATO bombing campaign against Yugoslavia, 80 percent of the surveillance shots were provided by U-2s.

The U-2's latest rival is the Global Hawk, an unmanned aerial vehicle (UAV) built by Northrop Grumman. Though the Air Force has made clear its desire to keep its U-2s flying until 2020, there are concerns that the current fleet will show its age well before that deadline, and that it will become harder to recruit competent pilots. But the Global Hawk's debut hasn't exactly knocked anyone's socks off. Of the six that have been built through 2002, three have crashed; the survivors were grounded. The Global Hawk's $50-million-per-plane price tag is also irking some congressmen, who say that initial cost projections were around $10 million. A U-2 costs about $53 million.

COULD EJECTION SEATS HAVE SAVED THE COLUMBIA ASTRONAUTS?

Few Air Force pilots would dare fly into combat without an ejection seat. Could ejection seats or escape pods have saved the Columbia *astronauts?*

Probably not. The *Columbia* disaster occurred within a matter of seconds, even milliseconds, which is hardly enough time for a seven-person crew to load into escape capsules. As for ejection seats, few pilots have ever survived popping out of a plane traveling in excess of 630 mph. When it broke apart, *Columbia* was hurtling along at Mach 18–eighteen times the speed of sound— so ejection would have brought certain death. In addition, the *Columbia* disintegrated at an altitude of 200,000 feet; 100,000 feet is generally considered to be the ceiling for a midair ejection to be survivable.

NASA has from time to time added escape devices to its shuttle fleet. For its first four flights, in 1981 and 1982, the *Columbia* featured ejection seats for the two-man crew. But these were removed as the shuttle crews expanded to five to seven members, and NASA deemed the shuttle safe enough to do without.

That aura of safety evaporated in the wake of the *Challenger* disaster in 1986, and NASA did add escape systems to the remaining shuttles. In the event of a disastrous takeoff, a side hatch can be jettisoned. A telescoping pole is then supposed to be extended beyond the wing, allowing the crew to attach their parachute rings and slide out into the clear. This escape plan can work only under limited circumstances, however. The shuttle cannot be much higher than 20,000 feet for the apparatus to work, and it must be in a controlled glide, not a steep ascent. Even then, the evacuation procedure could take upward of two minutes.

NASA revisited the prospect of adding escape pods or revamped ejection seats to the shuttle in 2001, when the agency's Safety Advisory Panel put together a report on the options. It concluded that "none of the options for crew escape can be funded within the current constraints on the space shuttle budget." The panel estimated that retrofitting the fleet with escape pods, which could survive drops of less than 200,000 feet, may have required eighteen months and nearly $1 billion. And there's a design problem: Escape pods require life-support mechanisms, and engineers would have to design a pod light enough to fit in the cargo bay.

NASA has considered adding escape systems to its orbital space plane, a next-generation vehicle slated to begin ferrying astronauts to and from the International Space Station around 2010. Last November, NASA awarded Lockheed Martin a $53 million contract to research escape options that might enable crews to abandon ship after a bungled takeoff—say, one in which critical heat-resistant tiles are damaged.

IS THERE REALLY SUCH A THING AS A WATER LANDING?

In July 1999, John F. Kennedy Jr., his wife, and her sister died when their plane crashed into the sea near Martha's Vineyard. Frequent fliers are familiar with instructions on what to do in case of what flight attendants euphemistically call a water landing. Is there such a thing as a water landing, and what are your chances of surviving one?

If you define a water landing as a controlled, if unplanned, descent onto water, as opposed to a simple crash, this is what aviators call a ditching. And yes, according to the U.S. Coast Guard, there is one ditching every day in U.S. waters. This includes helicopters and all fixed-wing aircraft—military, air carrier, corporate, and general aviation (a group that includes private planes such as the one Kennedy was flying). But there has never been a single ditching by a U.S.-flag commercial airline. Several non-U.S. airlines have experienced ditchings, with mixed results: Some passengers died and some survived.

The Aviation Consumer Action Project, a Ralph Nader group, has said that in an attempted water landing, a wide-body jet would "shatter like a raw egg dropped on pavement, killing most if not all passengers on impact, even in calm seas with well-trained pilots and good landing trajectories." Possibly because ditchings are both virtually nonexistent and virtually nonsurvivable, the Federal Aviation Administration does not require commercial pilots to train for them. Instead, it has various rules about how close planes must be to an airfield on land.

Any benefit from the procedures and precautions associated with the phrase *in the event of a water landing* are at this point purely theoretical.

HISTORY LESSONS

WHO WAS
**DR.
STRANGELOVE?**

HOW DID THE
UNITED STATES
GET A NAVAL BASE
IN CUBA?

WHERE DOES
**THE FIFTH
AMENDMENT**
COME FROM?

WHERE WAS
ABRAHAM
BORN?

WHY DOES
LOUISIANA
HAVE SUCH AN ODD
ELECTION SYSTEM?

WHAT KIND OF
TERRORISM
DID NORTH KOREA
SPONSOR?

WHO WAS DR. STRANGELOVE?

Stanley Kubrick's Dr. Strangelove—the icy technocrat who also happens to be a Nazi, the oddball defense strategist sexually aroused by the thought of nuclear war—is particularly creepy because he is an exaggeration of a familiar type. Which raises the question: Which real-life figures inspired Kubrick's creation?

Many incorrectly suspect that Henry Kissinger was Kubrick's model. While it is true that Kissinger had thick glasses and an even thicker accent, he was still a relatively obscure professor at Harvard in 1964, when the movie was originally released. (Kissinger didn't became national security advisor until 1969.) Of course, we cannot rule out the possibility that Kissinger subsequently modeled himself, consciously or subconsciously, after Strangelove.

America's best-known nuclear strategist in 1964 was American-born Herman Kahn, a physicist, RAND Corporation think tanker, and author of *On Thermonuclear War*. (Kahn's most famous argument was that some people would probably survive a nuclear war.) In the movie, Strangelove mentions an association with the Bland Corporation and argues that nuclear war is survivable. Kahn himself allowed that the character was "part Henry Kissinger, part myself, with a touch of Wernher von Braun."

Von Braun, the rocket scientist, was probably the source for Strangelove's poorly repressed Nazism. Von Braun developed the V-2 during World War II for Hitler, emigrated to the United States to create rockets for NASA, and became something of a national hero in the space agency's heyday of the 1960s. Mort Sahl once quipped that Von Braun's autobiography, *I Aimed for the Stars*, should have been subtitled "But Sometimes I Hit London."

Another influence was surely Edward Teller, the thickly accented physicist-cum-technocrat who developed the H-bomb. Teller was instrumental in scuttling Robert Oppenheimer's career, and many liberals considered him a scary warmonger. Finally, some say that Peter Sellers, the actor who played Strangelove, derived Strangelove's astonishing accent from Weegee, a well-known New York photographer of the period who emigrated from the Ukraine.

HOW DID THE UNITED STATES GET A NAVAL BASE IN CUBA?

What's the deal with the U.S. naval base in Guantánamo Bay, Cuba? How did the United States get a military base in a hostile Communist country?

The United States seized Guantánamo Bay and established a naval base there in 1898 during the Spanish-American War. Five years later, the United States and Cuba signed a lease giving Guantánamo Bay to the United States as a "coaling and naval station." The lease was required to implement the congressional Platt Amendment, which stipulated, among other things, that a naval base "at certain specified points to be agreed upon by the President of the United States" was required "to enable the United States to maintain the independence of Cuba."

In 1934, Cuba and the United States signed a treaty that gave the United States a perpetual lease to the area. The United States can't open a casino resort there, however: Private enterprise is banned under the terms of the treaty. The lease can be broken only by mutual agreement, so as a practical matter, Guantánamo Bay is U.S. property. It was there before Fidel Castro and will be there after him.

WHERE DOES THE FIFTH AMENDMENT COME FROM?

Former Enron chairman Kenneth Lay asserted his Fifth Amendment rights before a Senate committee in February 2002, "respectfully declining to answer" any of the committee's questions. What is the history behind and rationale for the Fifth Amendment right not to testify against oneself?

The Fifth Amendment to the U.S. Constitution provides that "no person . . . shall be compelled in any criminal case to be a witness against himself." The right was created in reaction to the excesses of the Courts of Star Chamber and High Commission—British courts of equity that operated from 1487 to 1641. These courts utilized the inquisitorial method of truth-seeking as opposed to the prosecutorial, meaning that prosecutors did not bear the burden of proving a case, but that sufficient "proof" came from browbeating confessions out of the accused.

These courts required the accused to answer any question put to him, without advance notice of his accusers, the charges against him, or the evidence amassed. With the abolition of the Courts of Star Chamber and High Commission, the common law courts of England incorporated this principle of *nemo tenetur*— that no man should be bound to accuse himself. By the eighteenth century, English law provided that neither confessions coerced during the trial nor pretrial confessions obtained through torture could be used. This was based on the belief that coerced confessions were inherently unreliable.

The right to be free from self-incrimination was established in nine state constitutions and was a tenet of the common law throughout most of the colonies before it appeared in the U.S. Constitution. Since then, the U.S. Supreme Court has expanded the Fifth Amendment to apply not only to criminal proceedings and pretrial proceedings in criminal matters, including interrogations in police stations, but also to "any other proceeding, civil or criminal, formal or informal, where his answers might incriminate him in future criminal proceedings." The law also prohibits prosecutors from making reference to a defendant's refusal to take the stand as probative of guilt. So long as the government is compelling potentially incriminating speech—before either a jury or a Senate committee—the right can be invoked.

WHERE WAS ABRAHAM BORN?

In April 2003, reporters attending the coalition talks in the Iraqi city of Ur noted that the summit took place in the "birthplace of Abraham." The phrase turned up in Associated Press and New York Times *reports and in stories on* Nightline *and* NBC Nightly News. *Was Abraham really born in Ur?*

This idea is understandably appealing because Abraham, through his sons Ishmael and Isaac, is considered the spiritual father of Jews, Christians, and Muslims. There's only one problem: The Bible doesn't say where Abraham was born.

Abraham first appears in the Bible in Genesis 11:27, which says that Terah, a descendant of Noah's son Shem, begets three children: Abram, Nahor, and Haran. (Abraham is called Abram at the moment, which means "the father is exalted." Not until he has a child of his own, decades later, will God change his name to Abraham, which means "father of many.") The next verse suggests that Abraham's youngest brother, Haran, was born in a place called Ur of the Chaldeans, where he dies (though not before fathering a son, Lot). It does not say that Abraham was born in Ur. As the text makes clear, Terah and his family were pastoral nomads, wandering from place to place for varying periods of time. So it's not inconceivable that Abraham and even Nahor might have been born someplace else. But where? And where was this place called Ur of the Chaldeans?

The answer is: We don't know. Despite two centuries of searching, there is no archaeological evidence that the events in the first five books of the Bible ever took place. As a result, everything in this question is conjecture.

The leading assumption among Jewish and Christian scholars

for the last century and a half has been that Ur of the Chaldeans refers to the ancient metropolis of Ur, capital of the mini-empire Sumer, which was indeed located in southeastern Iraq not far from Nasiryah. But this has problems. First, scholars now agree that the term *Chaldeans* is almost assuredly an anachronism, as it refers to a Semitic people who didn't show up in Ur until the seventh century B.C. Abraham, by contrast, would have lived 1,300 years earlier, closer to 2000 B.C. Second, nomadic people did not have a habit of settling alongside major cities.

Muslim commentators (and increasingly some Jewish and Christian ones) propose a radically different alternative. The Genesis story says that after leaving Ur of the Chaldeans, Terah and his family settle alongside the town of Harran, where Terah lives for sixty more years. Harran almost surely corresponds to the ancient trading center that is located today in southeastern Turkey, on the border with Syria. Considering that they were headed for Canaan, which is due west of Sumerian Ur, it makes no geographic sense that Terah and his family would travel 550 miles out of their way to southern Turkey. It seems more likely— as Muslim tradition suggests—that biblical Ur is actually in Upper Mesopotamia, closer to Harran. The town of Urfa, Turkey (notice the shared root with Ur), is less than 20 miles from Harran and contains an ancient cave where Muslim tradition says Abraham was born.

Regardless of how he got there, Christians, Jews, and Muslims agree that while he is in Harran, Abraham receives the command from God to "go forth from your native land and from your father's house to the land that I will show you." It is this call—holy to half the world's believers today—that sets him out toward the promised land and marks the symbolic start of monotheism.

WHY DOES LOUISIANA HAVE SUCH AN ODD ELECTION SYSTEM?

On Election Day 2002, Louisiana senator Mary Landrieu, a Democrat, faced off in a primary against eight other candidates, including

three major Republican challengers. Because she didn't win 50 per-
cent of the vote, she had to compete in a runoff—though all other
states had already picked their senators. How did Louisiana get such
an odd election system?

Every state, local, and congressional election in Louisiana is
decided by what's called an open primary. The rules are that all
candidates for a single office, regardless of party, appear on the
same ballot on election day, and all voters (again regardless of
party) can vote for any one of them. If no candidate wins 50 percent of the vote, a runoff between the top two vote-getters takes
place a month later. It's completely possible for the open primary
to produce a runoff between two Democrats or between two
Republicans. Ironically, the system that helped the GOP make
reelection difficult for Landrieu was put in place in 1975
by a Democrat, then governor (and now convicted felon) Edwin Edwards. In the 1970s, the South was still largely a Democratic stronghold, and incumbents like Edwards often faced their
stiffest challenges in Democratic primaries. So Edwards pushed
to do away with the traditional party primary system. The strategy
paid off. In 1975, facing weak opposition, he cruised to reelection.

The open primary has been criticized for forcing voters to go to
the polls twice in the space of a month, which tends to depress
turnout. Some academics contend that it favors incumbents (who
can afford to campaign twice), while others say it aids fringe candidates (who can get just enough votes to force a runoff). In 1991,
former Ku Klux Klan member David Duke used the open primary
system to force a runoff with Edwards. Thus originated the
famous bumper sticker: "Vote for the Crook: It's Important."

Louisiana's election system used to be even stranger. Until
1997, the open primary was held in October, which meant that if
a candidate got over 50 percent he could be elected to Congress
a month before the federal election day. The Supreme Court told
Louisiana to knock it off. So the state pushed its open primary
back a month, and now instead of electing candidates early, it
frequently elects them late. On December 7, 2002, Landrieu
won another Senate term with 52 percent of the vote.

WHAT KIND OF TERRORISM DID NORTH KOREA SPONSOR?

In 2003, the State Department officially cited North Korea as one of seven designated state sponsors of terrorism. Yet the Stalinist "Hermit Kingdom" is certainly no breeding ground for the likes of al-Qaida or Hezbollah. How exactly does North Korea sponsor terrorism?

According to the State Department, mainly by selling missile technology to the likes of Libya and Syria, two other members of the ominous list. There is also ample evidence that Kim Jong Il's regime has knowingly sold smaller weapons to separatist groups; three years ago, the Philippines publicly alleged that North Korea did an arms deal with the Moro Islamic Liberation Front. Such sales are believed to be one of North Korea's few sources of hard currency, along with counterfeiting and other criminal activities.

In terms of direct terrorist action, however, the Democratic People's Republic of Korea (as the nation is formally known) has been relatively quiet since 1987, when it's believed to have orchestrated the bombing of Korean Airlines Flight 858. That attack is thought to have been a tactic to scare tourists away from visiting the 1988 Summer Olympics in Seoul; Kim Jong Il was miffed that his country had not been asked to cohost the games. North Korean operatives were also behind a 1983 attempt on the life of South Korean President Chun Doo-Hwan, who was sched-uled to visit a memorial in Rangoon, Burma (now Myanmar). A traffic delay may have saved the president's life: The timed bombs went off before his arrival, killing seventeen South Korean digni-taries instead.

South Korea also believes that its northern neighbor was behind the 1996 assassination of a South Korean diplomat in Vladivostok, Russia. The killing closely followed a warning from Pyongyang that it would take action if South Korea did not repa-triate the bodies of several North Korean spies. Every year, the State Department also mentions North Korea's harboring of four members of the Japanese Communist League's Red Army Fac-tion. These terrorists were involved in the 1970 hijacking of a Japan Airlines jet, sometimes referred to as the Yodogo Incident.

They flew the plane to North Korea, hoping to found an operational base from which they could foment a worldwide proletariat revolution. These Red Army members (originally nine in number) were allegedly later responsible for ordering the kidnappings of several Japanese citizens and spiriting them away to North Korea in the hopes of brainwashing them into becoming Communist loyalists. Japan still demands the extradition of the surviving four hijackers, but Pyongyang shows no signs of relenting after all these years.

HIGH TECH

WHAT IS
MOORE'S LAW?

CAN YOU
PATENT COMMON
FEATURES
OF THE
INTERNET?

WHO PATROLS
THE INTERNET
FOR VIRUSES?

WHAT'S THE
DIFFERENCE BETWEEN A
VIRUS AND A
WORM?

CAN YOU VIOLATE
COPYRIGHT
LAW
WITH A MAGIC
MARKER?

HOW CAN
CELL PHONES
REVEAL YOUR
LOCATION?

WHAT IS MOORE'S LAW?

In a September 1999 issue of Science *magazine, a scientist wrote that the computer industry was "in serious danger" of violating Moore's law. What is Moore's law?*

Moore's law is really just a prediction that the processing power of the state-of-the-art computer chip will double every eighteen months. It's named after computer engineer Gordon Moore, a cofounder of the Intel Corporation. In 1965, Moore observed that since the invention of integrated circuits (or microchips) in 1959, the number of transistors that a chip of constant surface area could hold had doubled once every year or two. (Integrated circuits are the basic units of computer logic and memory, and transistors are the on-off switches that allow digital information to be transmitted, processed, and stored. The more transistors you can pack on a circuit, the more powerful the circuit becomes.) Moore simply predicted that this pattern would continue.

Even though it's not really a law, Moore's prediction has held true for the past three decades. In fact, its hallowed status has made it self-fulfilling: Chipmakers and industry analysts now set their goals and forecasts based on Moore's law. And because chip prices have decreased even as capacity has risen, the computer processing power available to consumers at a given price has doubled even more quickly.

Since Moore's law depends on the continuous shrinking of transistors, scientists generally agree that it will eventually be violated. Previous predictions that it would break down have thus far proved incorrect, though, and most scientists expect Moore's law to hold for at least ten to fifteen more years.

CAN YOU PATENT COMMON FEATURES OF THE INTERNET?

In 2003, telecom giant SBC sent cease-and-desist letters to hundreds of website operators, accusing them of infringing on an SBC patent covering frames, those stationary menus that innumerable websites employ to help users. SBC said individual infringers owed it licensing payments ranging from $527 to $16.6 million per year. Does SBC own such a patent? And if so, how was it allowed to patent such a seemingly obvious feature?

The answer to the first question is yes. SBC secured its first frame patent in 1999 and a second in 2002. It's standard practice for large corporations to quickly patent the work of their engineering corps, even when the exact nature of future applications may be uncertain. It's a process that only wealthy players like SBC can afford to engage in on a regular basis—legal fees alone can cost tens of thousands of dollars.

How could the government let the company patent such a common feature as frames? Keep in mind that software patents are a relatively new phenomenon. Until the early 1980s, the courts generally considered software to be nothing more elaborate than applied mathematics, and thus not patentable. That's why the geeks behind such pre-eighties computing wonders as the first-ever database, word processor, and spreadsheet missed the boat: An inventor has just one year from the first public use, printed publication, or commercial promotion of an invention to file for a patent.

That anti-software bias changed slowly, as attorneys became more savvy about describing the unique challenges of programming and judges got hip to the complexities of coding. In 1996, the U.S. Patent and Trademark Office (USPTO) issued its first guidelines intended to "facilitate the patenting of computer software." Two years later, the federal case *State Street Bank & Trust Co. v. Signature Financial Group* affirmed a relatively low bar for the patenting of software, listing a wide range of criteria under which programs could be considered to provide a "useful, tangible, and concrete result"—a patent prerequisite. Essentially, *State*

Street said that any software with a practical use had a good shot at passing muster. Computer-related patent applications nearly doubled.

Problem is, the USPTO was ill prepared to handle the flurry. Its personnel were not particularly computer literate nor accustomed to researching programming history. To receive a patent, an invention must be both nonobvious and new. Critics say USPTO's staffers didn't possess the technical expertise to decide the first issue, and they didn't know enough about computing literature to resolve the latter. When researching a patent application, the USPTO is supposed to seek examples of "prior art," or similar inventions from the past that might disprove the novelty of the subject in question. Typically, this involves looking through peer-reviewed journals and other traditional scientific sources. But computing knowledge has been disseminated in much more haphazard ways—through mailing lists, at open-source conferences, in university dorms. The USPTO just wasn't clued in to where it should look for the patent realm's equivalent of exculpatory evidence.

Thus many thousands of patents may have been granted to software bits that would have failed a proper prior-art test. *San Jose Mercury News* columnist Dan Gillmor recently asked his readers to dredge up prior instances of intrasite frame navigation in order to lampoon SBC's claims. Dozens of suggestions have poured in, stretching back to Apple's Reagan-era HyperCard and a 1994 manual for IBM's BookManager Library Reader.

Patents are not written in stone, and many are successfully overturned amid legal challenges. In 1994, for example, the USPTO overturned a patent it had given to Compton's New Media, which covered a broad technique whereby data is retrieved from CD-ROMs. Had it been allowed to stand, the patent might have squelched the development of digital media, since potential competitors would have owed Compton's millions in licensing fees.

And just last August, a federal judge rejected British Telecommunications' bizarre claim that the entire Internet violated its 1989 patent on the concept of the hyperlink. BT sued the Internet service provider Prodigy, claiming that it owed massive licensing fees for hosting pages that included hyperlinks. U.S. District Judge Colleen McMahon dismissed BT's case summarily, finding that the patent did not accurately describe the Internet. (The BT patent included language referring to a central computer, which the Internet lacks.) SBC, by the way, owns Prodigy.

WHO PATROLS THE INTERNET FOR VIRUSES?

Every few months, a new virus chews through the world's computer systems. What government agency monitors the Internet for attacks?

The federal National Infrastructure Protection Center (NIPC) coordinates computer crime investigations in the United States by collecting information from law enforcement agencies, the military, the private sector, and state and local governments. The NIPC's mission to deter, detect, and investigate malicious acts that threaten the Internet also extends to rest of the nation's critical infrastructure, which includes the telecommunications grid, the electrical power system, the banking and finance system, oil and gas distribution, government operations, transportation systems, and water systems. The NIPC's mission was laid out in a presidential directive issued by President Clinton in 1998.

The NIPC is housed in the headquarters of the Federal Bureau of Investigation, and it operates under the authority of the attorney general. It divides Internet attacks into three categories: unstructured threats (from individuals and hackers), structured threats (from organized crime or terrorists), and national security threats (from foreign governments). Once the NIPC has determined the source and scope of an attack, it coordinates the response with national security agencies, law enforcement, or the private sector.

WHAT'S THE DIFFERENCE BETWEEN A VIRUS AND A WORM?

*Palyh, an Internet contagion that hit in 2003, masqueraded as an
e-mail from Microsoft technical support. Some writers termed Palyh
a virus, others a worm. What's the difference?*

It's all about reproduction. Like their parasitic namesakes, computer viruses need to attach to hosts in order to survive. A virus
latches onto a program such as Word or Excel, modifying the host
(by inserting its code into the application's code) and replicating
itself when the host program is active. A virus can thus spread all
over a single user's machine but needs help to infect other computers. Unwitting humans can do the trick with an infected
floppy disk, but the more common approach is for a virus to
spread through a Trojan horse.

As the *Iliad*-derived name suggests, a Trojan is a delivery program
that appears benign but actually carries a virus-filled payload. In
the case of Palyh, the executable attachment masquerading as a
Microsoft patch was a textbook Trojan. Opening the file would
not update your operating system, but rather infect your computer with Palyh while sending additional Palyh-laden Trojans to
the e-mail addresses stored on your computer. Like many other
Trojan-borne viruses, Palyh had an expiration date—it was no
longer active after May 31, 2003.

Worms are a smaller subset of viruses. They can also propagate
via Trojans, but once a worm infects your computer, it acts as a
stand-alone program and does not require a host in order to survive and reproduce, seeking instead to copy itself without your
help. Worms can do this because they are generally network
aware—that is, they automatically seek network connections over
which to spread, searching for security holes and other weak-
nesses. These pests are considered more loathsome than viruses,
especially in networked environments. If one unwary employee
clicks on an infected attachment, every machine in the company
may soon be tainted. If that same doofus clicks on a traditional
virus, his or her coworkers may still need to open the resulting Trojan-bearing e-mails for the virus to spread. According to

anti-virus vendor Symantec, Palyh looked for shared folders to infect and thus deserved the worm appellation.

These definitions aren't written in stone, and hybrids are common. Also up for debate is the origin of the term *worm*. One school of thought holds that it dates back to the 1960s, when computer code ran on reel-to-reel tapes. This ostensibly gave rise to *tapeworm*, later shortened to its current length. The other theory is that the word comes from the 1975 John Brunner novel *The Shockwave Rider*, a proto-cyberpunk classic. As for *virus*, it's pretty much agreed that the term's father is computer scientist Fred Cohen, author of the landmark 1984 paper "Computer Viruses: Theory and Experiments."

CAN YOU VIOLATE COPYRIGHT LAW WITH A MAGIC MARKER?

Sony is selling CDs outfitted with Key2Audio, a technology that prevents you from burning a copy on your home computer or converting the songs into MP3 files. Hackers, in turn, foiled Key2Audio by scribbling on the discs with felt-tip pens. Were they running afoul of federal copyright laws?

Yes, but the feds didn't exactly knock down doors in search of pre-teens ripping off Shakira's latest opus. Section 1201 of the 1998 Digital Millennium Copyright Act (DMCA) makes it illegal to circumvent any copy-protection scheme. Since Key2Audio was designed to prevent piracy, the Magic Marker trick qualifies as such a measure.

Yet most hackers needn't fear the DMCA's stiff criminal penalties, which include up to ten years behind bars and $1 million in fines. A circumventer is unlikely to be prosecuted unless he's caught selling the copied CDs. Those who spread the Magic Marker method via Internet news groups or articles are on shakier legal ground, however. Section 1201 also includes a broadly worded trafficking provision that forbids the dissemination of copyright-shirking methods. Writers who described the method could be prosecuted if their work is judged to have no raison d'être other than to aid budding pirates. Media outlets are in the clear, but the geeks who first shared the felt-tip techniques on alt.music news groups could be in hot water.

Bonus Explainer: Another player in the Key2Audio drama who put himself in greater danger of feeling the DMCA's wrath is the smart-ass who recently tried to sell a Sharpie marker on eBay. Describing the marker, he wrote: "For the purpose of scribbling on Sony CDs." That could have been construed as trafficking a circumvention device, a no-no according to Section 1201.

HOW CAN CELL PHONES REVEAL YOUR LOCATION?

As part of its investigation into Jayson Blair's journalistic sins, The New York Times pored over the reporter's cell-phone records. According to the paper, the records indicated that Blair often falsified his whereabouts, claiming to be reporting from West Virginia or Maryland while still in New York. How do cell phones reveal their users' physical locations, and how did the Times get its mitts on Blair's records?

The simplest means of fixing a customer's location is to figure out which tower a call was routed through. When you ring someone up on your mobile, the signal seeks out the closest cell-phone tower. The tower that handled the call is typically logged (and stored indefinitely) on the wireless provider's computers, though it's not noted on the customer's monthly bill. In an urban area, each tower covers an area of approximately 1 to 2 square miles, so a caller's general location is fairly easy to pinpoint.

A newer, more precise method of tracking cell-phone users is via satellite. Many new handsets are equipped with Global Positioning System chips, which determine a caller's coordinates by receiving signals beamed down from a satellite array. The chip factors together the signals' different arrival times to calculate the phone's coordinates, using a mathematical process known as trilateration. GPS-enabled phones are becoming ubiquitous because of Enhanced 911, a Federal Communications Commission rule mandating that emergency operators must be able to trace wireless calls; 95 percent of cell phones must be E911 compliant by the end of 2005. At present, however, GPS data is typically not recorded for nonemergency purposes, unless the user has explicitly signed up for a location-based service.

Location data extrapolated from tower records is frequently used in criminal cases. It was vital, for example, to the prosecution of David Westerfield, who was convicted of murdering 7-year-old Danielle van Dam in San Diego, California. The killer's cell-phone usage revealed a bizarre travel pattern in the two days following the girl's disappearance, including a suspicious trip to the desert. In cases like this, wireless providers will not release a user's records without a court order, save for rare instances in which a kidnapping has taken place and time is of the essence.

The Blair situation, by contrast, does not involve a criminal proceeding. It is likely that he was using a *Times*-issued cell phone, a common perk at the Gray Lady. The newspaper, then, was merely requesting to view its own records, rather than those of a third party. No federal law specifically addresses the right of an employer to view an employee's cell-phone records, though case law on workplace surveillance indicates that Blair likely had no reasonable expectation of privacy while using a company phone.

In the absence of concrete legal guidelines, the decision whether to release the records without a subpoena comes down to the wireless provider's whim.

GUNS AND AMMO

WHAT IS A **PAINT BOMB?**

WHAT'S THE **NUCLEAR TRIAD?**

WHAT'S A **NUCLEAR-CAPABLE MISSILE?**

HOW DO YOU **DESTROY A MISSILE?**

HOW DOES **REPROCESSING FUEL RODS** HELP BUILD **NUCLEAR BOMBS?**

WHAT ARE **RUBBER BULLETS?**

WHAT IS A PAINT BOMB?

A Dutch boat offering offshore abortions docked in Wladyslawowo, Poland, in June 2003, where pro-life demonstrators greeted it with a barrage of stones and paint bombs. The same month, two paint bombs were thrown at the home of an official in Northern Ireland. What is a paint bomb?

A low-tech favorite of student protesters and sectarian thugs alike, particularly in Europe, paint bombs vary in both design and destructive force. The simplest, least damaging ones are simply paint-filled versions of that prankster classic the water balloon. Do-it-yourselfers must jury-rig a pumping device; simply pouring paint into a balloon won't work, due to lack of pressure. It's also critical to thin the paint a bit and to avoid brands containing solvents that could dissolve the balloon's skin before launch.

Another fairly innocuous method is to poke two holes in an egg, empty out the contents, and use the remaining shell as a bomb casing. The very thinned-out ordnance is often poured in from a Tabasco bottle, ideal for its narrow spout.

These bombs are often used by protesters to vandalize emblems they abhor. During an April demonstration in Mexico City, for example, antiwar protesters hurled paint bombs at several Burger King and KFC franchises, as a token of their displeasure with the Bush administration's Iraq policy. And several of the Tiananmen Square protesters were handed lengthy prison sentences for splattering portraits of Mao Zedong.

A more dangerous paint-bomb variant is a staple of street violence in Northern Ireland, especially during the annual "marching season." There, militants fill empty liquor bottles with thin paint or printer's ink and hurl the contraptions at rival churches, objectionable murals, or the homes of adversaries. Catholic hooligans prefer to coat their targets in the green, white, and orange of the Irish flag, while their Protestant rivals use the red, white, and blue of the Union Jack. Flying shards of glass can cause more than just superficial damage, of course, especially when such a projectile is tossed into a living room.

Perhaps the most dangerous paint bomb is a seldom used, nonprojectile version that consists of nothing more than a can of paint and some dry ice. When the ice is mixed in and the lid resealed, pressure quickly builds, eventually creating a volcano-like effect. Far too heavy to throw very far, and prone to sudden detonation, the dry-ice recipe is a risky, albeit potentially devastating approach. The lid can wreak havoc when sent aloft by the explosion.

WHAT'S THE NUCLEAR TRIAD?

After President George W. Bush and Russian president Vladimir Putin announced plans to reduce the number of their countries' nuclear warheads in November 2001, a former Clinton administration official told The Washington Post: *"We're breaking what had been an effective sound barrier in the arms control world, which is the 2,000 number. That had always been the holy grail—if you go below 2,000 [the theory went], you'll lose the strategic triad." Okay, but what's the strategic triad?*

The United States can deliver a nuclear attack by land, by sea, or by air: with land-based intercontinental ballistic missiles, sea-based submarine-launched ballistic missiles, and airborne strategic bombers. That's the triad. Since the 1960s, U.S. nuclear strategy has relied on it to fulfill the pledge of mutually assured destruction: that the country could survive a surprise first strike by the Soviet Union (or any other nuclear power) and then respond with a devastating strike of its own. Each leg of the triad is supposed to be large enough to have a deterrent effect.

The theory is that a first strike against the United States could not hope to destroy all three legs of the triad at once, and even if two of the three legs of the triad are destroyed, the third can still inflict a retaliatory strike. In addition, having three legs protects against the risk that a new technology (such as a missile-defense system) could threaten the viability of a single delivery system.

WHAT'S A NUCLEAR-CAPABLE MISSILE?

In January 2003, India test-launched a short-range Agni I missile, described in press reports as nuclear capable. What's a nuclear-capable missile?

At a minimum, any missile that can tote the crudest of nuclear devices. Arms experts estimate that the least sophisticated nuclear warheads, like those in India's arsenal, will weigh a minimum of 500 kilograms. To be deemed "nuclear capable," then, a missile must simply be able to deliver the 500-kilogram payload to a target. The category is often further limited to missiles with ranges greater than 300 kilometers, as that is considered the smallest possible distance between two nuclear combatants. (The distance and carrying standards are laid down by the 33-nation Missile Technology Control Regime, a consortium that restricts the export of flying rockets.)

For an advanced member of the nuclear club, like the United States, the weight issue is a rather piddling one. The American military has the technology to miniaturize nuclear arms virtually at will, as evidenced by the number of "backpack" bombs in the Cold War arsenal. India, on the other hand, is still fiddling with fat, unwieldy contraptions and thus must piggyback its nukes on massive rockets like the Agni I. (Many observers believe that Pakistan, which purchases its conventional missiles from North Korea, may be slightly ahead of its neighbor in the subcontinent's arms race, at least in terms of getting well below the 500-kilogram benchmark.) The lighter the warhead, the better the chance a military has of shoehorning it into a stealthier, more agile projectile, such as a Cruise or Tomahawk missile. The U.S. arsenal boasts nuclear-tipped versions of both.

Were a nuclear confrontation to break out between the two powers, chances are the weapons would be delivered via aircraft rather than rockets. Test launches make for impressive gunboat diplomacy, but the failure rates for ballistic missiles make them a dicey gamble, especially for a still nascent nuclear nation. And of course a missile can't be recalled once launched, no matter how successful last-minute diplomatic talks may be. It's marginally safer to have the bombers circling.

HOW DOES REPROCESSING FUEL RODS HELP BUILD NUCLEAR BOMBS?

Among North Korea's feather-ruffling moves in April 2003 was the claim that the country has reprocessed 8,000 spent nuclear fuel rods. What does rod reprocessing have to do with building fresh nukes?

It's basically the poor man's way of obtaining plutonium, the substance most prized for the fabrication of nuclear weapons because of its relative stability. The fuel rods in question are leftovers from North Korea's reactors, which were ostensibly built for nonmilitary purposes. Such rods are initially filled with enriched uranium— that is, uranium with a relatively high content of the fissile uranium-235 isotope. Naturally occurring uranium is approximately 99.3 percent uranium-238, which doesn't do the trick when inserted into a reactor. Enriched uranium has been "purified" in order to up the uranium-235 percentage to about 5 percent.

When a fuel rod is made, enriched uranium is baked into inch-long pellets and inserted into metal tubes. In the belly of a reactor, the atoms of this fuel split apart, releasing tremendous amounts of energy in the form of heat. That heat turns the surrounding water into steam, which in turn pushes a turbine. During this process, the uranium-238 converts into plutonium-239, which is ideal for weapons production. However, since civilian reactors are designed to keep pumping until all the fuel's spent, the morphing doesn't stop there. Some of those plutonium-239 atoms absorb an additional neutron and become plutonium-240. The new isotope isn't fissile and thus not what military engineers crave.

After a year or two, the fuel rods are tapped out. They're often transported to a nearby water tank, where they cool down for a while—the irradiation process creates so much heat that rods need one to three years to become sufficiently chilly. That's when reprocessing can commence. The simplest approach is to dissolve the rods in nitric acid, a technique known as the purex process. The end result is approximately 96 percent uranium, 1 percent plutonium, and 3 percent assorted toxic by-products. (The ratio of Pu240 to Pu239 in the resulting plutonium depends on a variety of factors, including the percentage of uranium-235 in the pellet and the length of time the rod was used.) Proponents of nuclear energy argue that recycling the rods reduces waste, since the plutonium and uranium can be reused as fuel.

The downside is that the resulting plutonium can also be used for more nefarious projects. The U.S. Department of Energy officially defines weapons-grade plutonium as that containing at least 93 percent of the fissile plutonium-239 isotope. (The rest can be nonfissile Pu240.) But even crude reactor grades—those that contain less than 80 percent Pu239—can still pack a wallop. There's also no way of knowing whether the North Koreans operate their reactors specifically to minimize the conversion of plutonium-239 to plutonium-240, which would produce truly menacing nuclear material.

HOW DO YOU DESTROY A MISSILE?

In February 2003, weapons inspector Hans Blix said Iraq had promised to destroy its arsenal of Al-Samoud 2 missiles. What's the procedure for deep-sixing a warhead-less missile?

It's a good deal more complicated than just loosening some bolts. Missiles like the Al-Samoud 2 are powered by systems not too terribly different from the space shuttle's internal engines. They're filled with highly compressed, flammable liquid propellants, which must be encased in ultrastrong steel-and-aluminum casings, sans screws, for safety reasons. Though it's technically feasible to drill holes in the weapon and drain out the fuel, it's too hazardous to be practical in most cases—one errant maneuver and the defuser will be vaporized.

Instead, explosives demolition experts are usually called in. Components that can be safely removed, such as gyroscopes, are first stripped away. Then the specialists give the design a thorough once-over, seeking out critical pressure points that will hopefully buckle when blasted. Shaped cutting charges are placed on these points and remotely detonated from a safe distance. The remains are then crushed with a steamroller, to guarantee that they cannot be salvaged from a scrap heap. It's particularly important to puree the most hard-to-find engine parts, such as thrust regulators and gas generators. Smaller components may also be melted in furnaces, just to make sure.

WHAT ARE RUBBER BULLETS?

In 2000, police and soldiers quelled rebellion with rubber bullets. Israeli soldiers shot them at Palestinian rioters. Bolivian soldiers shot them at farmers protesting the destruction of coca crops. Los Angeles police aimed them at anarchists disrupting the Democratic National Convention. Just what are rubber bullets, and what are they designed to do?

The term *rubber bullets* is used for about seventy-five types of less-than-lethal devices designed to deliver a stinging blow that incapacitates but does not kill or penetrate flesh as do regular metal bullets.

The first less-than-lethal bullets appeared in the 1880s, when Singapore police shot sawed-off broom handles at rioters. By the 1960s, riot control police in Singapore, Malaysia, and Hong Kong were using more sophisticated wooden bullets. (Wooden bullets still in use today are called knee-knockers.) British colonists brought the idea back home to England, where they replaced the wood—which could shatter and possibly penetrate—with rubber. Tens of thousands of rounds of rubber bullets were fired by British soldiers at citizens of Northern Ireland starting in the 1970s. By the 1980s the British had switched to more accurate plastic bullets, solid polyvinyl chloride cylinders about 4 inches long and 1½ inches wide. The bullets are supposed to be shot at the lower half of the body; about nineteen people have been killed by them in Northern Ireland mostly because of injury to the head. Numerous groups from the European Parliament to Human Rights Watch have called for a ban on plastic bullets.

In response to the Palestinian uprising that started in the late 1980s, the Israeli military developed its own rubber bullets designed to disperse crowds, to injure but not kill. These small rubber-coated metal pellets are supposed to be shot from a distance of about 130 feet and to be aimed at people's legs. But they can be lethal if shot at the head at closer range, and dozens of Palestinians have died from such injuries. Israeli political scientist Yaron Ezrahi entitled his book examining moral conflicts in his country *Rubber Bullets*.

Rubber bullets were introduced in the United States to quell antiwar and civil rights demonstrators in the 1960s. A fatality in 1971 stopped their use until their reintroduction in the late 1980s. Though famously deployed against protesters, they are most often used by individual police officers to subdue armed, mentally ill people. The most common kinds are the beanbag bullet, a cloth pouch with about 40 grams of lead shot that delivers the equivalent of a punch from Lennox Lewis, and a plastic cylinder like that used in Northern Ireland. There have been at least seven known fatalities in the United States and Canada from the weapons.

CONSPIRACY THEORIES

DID THE
UNITED STATES
EXPOSE IRAQI CIVILIANS
TO RADIATION?

HOW DO
SUPER-INTELLIGENT
BILLBOARDS
SPY ON YOUR
CAR RADIO?

WHAT'S A
RATLINE?

WAS
BARBERSHOP
RIGHT ABOUT
ROSA PARKS?

HOW DID COMPOSER
**PIERRE
BOULEZ**
BECOME A
TERRORISM SUSPECT?

IS THERE
COCAINE
ON YOUR MONEY?

DID THE UNITED STATES EXPOSE IRAQI CIVILIANS TO RADIATION?

Saddam Hussein's Iraqi government long claimed that uranium-tipped American shells used during the first Gulf War were to blame for an upsurge in cancer deaths and birth defects among Iraqi civilians. Did the United States expose Iraqis to radiation?

The United States did indeed shower Iraq with well over 300 tons' worth of depleted uranium (DU) ordnance during the first Gulf War. Because of its high density, DU—a by-product of the uranium enrichment process at nuclear reactors—is particularly effective in piercing armored vehicles. DU shells incinerate on impact, leaving behind a dusty residue that is primarily composed of the isotope uranium-238. The first Gulf War marked the first widespread use of DU ordnance; it has since been fired in Kosovo and Bosnia-Herzegovina by NATO forces. An estimated fifteen nations, primarily in the West, are believed to possess DU weapons.

Many scientists fear that this dust, when inhaled or ingested via contaminated water, emits radiation inside the lungs or lymph nodes, leading to cancer and other severe ailments. Iraq's health ministry claimed that cancer rates soared by 400 percent after 1991, and victims of Gulf War syndrome in the United States and Europe have frequently ascribed their maladies to DU exposure. In 2001, Doug Rokke, former head of the Pentagon's Depleted Uranium Project, told the British Parliament that a fifth of his Gulf War team—which examined Iraqi vehicles hit by DU fire—had since died of various lung diseases. During a later visit to Baghdad, Representative David Bonior, D-Mich., characterized DU's long-term impact on Iraq as "horrific and barbaric."

The Pentagon has dismissed a direct link between DU residue and cancer. It often points to a 1999 RAND Corporation study that monitored the health of Gulf War veterans exposed to DU and concluded that no link between kidney disease and DU had been found. The Department of Defense also argues that DU dust is less toxic than naturally occurring uranium, of which there is typically 2 to 4 tons per square mile of topsoil. A British researcher has theorized that any uptick in Iraqi cancer rates is due not to DU pollution but rather to Saddam Hussein's use of sulfur mustard gas during the Iran-Iraq War.

The World Health Organization published its own report in April of 2001. The organization agreed that a link between DU exposure and cancer has yet to be established but cautioned that its study relied heavily on military data. "Some scientists would like to see a larger body of independently—i.e., nonmilitary—funded studies to confirm the current viewpoint," the WHO paper stated. Researchers should have plenty of time to accumulate the necessary data; the half-life for uranium-238 is 4.4 billion years.

HOW DO SUPER-INTELLIGENT BILLBOARDS SPY ON YOUR CAR RADIO?

A *new breed of electronic billboards that can alter their text and graphics every hour monitors the radio-listening habits of passing motorists. According to* The New York Times, *the billboards' sensors detect "radiation leakage that is emitted when antennae are tuned to a given radio station." Is your car stereo a Chernobyl waiting to happen?*

Though the phrase *radiation leakage* may conjure up some rather nasty images, the phenomenon is relatively benign. The signals emitted by radio towers are in essence a form of radiation, commonly referred to as radio frequency radiation (RFR). These electromagnetic waves are picked up by your car's antenna and then converted into recognizable noise—music, talk shows, and the like—by the tuner. Cheap car-radio antennae—known as monopoles—are not particularly efficient mechanisms, and thus not all of the RFR is converted into useful content. Antennae leak a significant amount back into the surroundings, and this is what is picked up by the billboards' sensors. Because radio stations broadcast relatively strong narrowband signals, those sensors can differentiate the passerby's radio choices from the countless other waves that emanate throughout the universe. NASA's SETI program, which is searching for signs of extraterrestrial intelligence by looking for narrowband signals, operates according to similar principles.

None of this means that you should fear your car antenna as a health hazard. RFR is a low-frequency type of radiation, and is thus nonionizing—that is, it will not alter the molecules that form your body. There is some scientific debate as to whether long-term low-level exposure to RFR and other low-frequency electromagnetic waves can cause health problems. But the controversy centers on radio towers and other transmitters, not car-radio antennae.

HOW DID COMPOSER PIERRE BOULEZ BECOME A TERRORISM SUSPECT?

New York Times *columnist Bob Herbert wrote that in November 2001, a malicious joke led Swiss police to temporarily confiscate the passport and train ticket of 75-year-old French composer and conductor Pierre Boulez. What was the joke, and who played it?*

Zurich police added Boulez's name to their list of terrorism suspects six years ago "after a critic who had written a scathing review of one of his performances claimed to have received a threatening phone call alluding to a possible bomb attack," London's *Guardian* reported. Boulez's spokeswoman later told *The New York Times:* "The person who called may have said he was Mr. Boulez. It was evidently a joke in extremely bad taste, but the critic reported it to the police, and Mr. Boulez's name was entered into their files."

As a result, Boulez's name came up as a potential threat during a routine police check of hotel guest lists in November. Three policemen woke Boulez from his five-star hotel in Basel, Switzerland, during a predawn raid. They confiscated his passport for three hours. The chief of police has written Boulez an apology, and a police spokesman told the *Guardian*: "I hope it won't stop him coming back here again. I understand a lot of Swiss people like his music."

For the record, the BBC reported the story slightly differently, saying that "it was not a case of mistaken identity. In the revolutionary 1960s, it seems that Boulez said that opera houses should be blown up, comments which the Swiss felt made him a potential security threat." The *Times* says Boulez "was not being literal, and that was not what prompted" the investigation.

WAS <u>BARBERSHOP</u> RIGHT ABOUT ROSA PARKS?

Reverend Jesse Jackson was irked by the film Barbershop, *in which a character played by Cedric the Entertainer complains that Rosa Parks gets too much credit for the 1955–56 Montgomery bus boycott. Parks, he says, is deified because she was affiliated with the NAACP; worthier pioneers were simply forgotten. Is the movie's history lesson accurate?*

Pretty much. Nine months before Parks famously refused to relinquish her bus seat to a white passenger, 15-year-old Claudette Colvin was arrested for the identical crime. On March 2, 1955, Colvin boarded a bus opposite Martin Luther King Jr.'s church on Montgomery's Dexter Avenue. She was seated next to a pregnant African-American woman known only as Mrs. Hamilton. As the bus became crowded, the driver requested that the pair stand so whites could sit. Both refused, although another black passenger eventually let Hamilton take his place. Colvin, angry over the arrest of a classmate who'd been accused of raping a white woman, stood firm and was charged with misconduct, resisting arrest, and violating municipal segregation laws.

Colvin was later found guilty and placed on probation. Though her plight attracted national attention, local black leaders were reluctant to use Colvin as a test case. She became pregnant by a much older man soon after the arrest, which scandalized the deeply religious community. The white press, they assumed, would flaunt Colvin's illegitimate pregnancy as a means of undermining any boycott. Some historians also argue that civil rights leaders, who were predominately middle-class, were uneasy with Colvin's impoverished background.

On October 21 of that same year, 18-year-old Mary Louise Smith was also arrested for defying a bus driver's orders to relinquish her seat. She was upset after being stiffed for $11 by her employer, a white woman for whom she worked as a maid. Yet again, Montgomery activists were hesitant to turn a teenager's arrest into a cause célèbre. It is widely believed that rumors concerning Smith's father's alcoholism were a turnoff. (Smith vehemently denies that her father drank.)

Parks, a 42-year-old seamstress and secretary for the local chapter of the NAACP, was not arrested until December 1, 1955. At last report, Colvin lived in the Bronx, working as a nurse's aide. Smith still lives in Montgomery, in virtual anonymity.

IS THERE COCAINE ON YOUR MONEY?

Ira Glasser, executive director of the American Civil Liberties Union, took out a large ad in The New York Times *in December 1998 asking, "Did you know that there's a three out of four chance that the money you're carrying could be legally confiscated?" His argument was that 75 percent of American currency is contaminated with cocaine. Was he right?*

Glasser was correct that paper money is commonly contaminated with cocaine. Studies published by Argonne National Laboratories, the FBI, and the *Journal of Forensic Sciences* have placed the number between 70 and 100 percent. But the government is not allowed to seize your wallet just because it contains contaminated money. In 1994, a U.S. Circuit Court held that ordinary money contains enough cocaine to attract a drug-sniffing dog. Accordingly, the court ruled that a drug-dog hit does not count as probable cause to seize money.

Until recently, the prevalence of coke-contaminated money actually *checked* police power. Some defendants discovered to have coke residue on their hands argued successfully that it came from contaminated bills. Unfortunately for future defendants, however, the 1997 Argonne study found that handling a contaminated bill doesn't transmit coke to your hands. (That was the apparent rationale for the study.) For one thing, coke molecules are generally embedded in the fibers of a bill, where they won't rub off on your hands. For another, the average amount of coke on a bill is tiny, perhaps 6 to 10 nanograms (one billionth of a gram). Other studies estimate there are bigger things to worry about: Between 7 and 42 percent of bills contain revolting bacteria of all sorts, including fecal bacteria.

Where does the coke come from? A few bills get dusted with the drug when they are used to wrap crack rock, are handled by technicians who cut and package cocaine powder, or are rolled as sniffing straws. The FBI speculates that ATMs, which are filled with brushes and rollers, distribute the coke through the rest of the money supply.

WHAT'S A RATLINE?

In a July 2003 briefing, General Tommy R. Franks defended an earlier raid near the Syria-Iraq border that killed two civilians. The attack, he said, was designed to disrupt a ratline that was being used to shuttle Baathist officials in and out of Iraq. What are the origins of the word?

Ratline is a nautical term, referring to small lengths of horizontal cord that run between the shrouds, several strong ropes that affix the top of a mast to the vessel's sides. The ratlines serve as crude ladder rungs, allowing the crew to scale the mast when necessary. In bygone days, scampering up the ratlines was a last, desperate recourse for sailors on sinking ships, at least if they were unfortunate enough to have missed out on the lifeboats. As a result, *ratline* became a synonym for last-ditch escape route.

When used in the military context, the word most often connotes an enemy's getaway route, particularly one that's clandestine or passes through an otherwise secure area. The most famous example is the post–World War II ratline that smuggled Nazis and their allies from Europe to South America. The underground was operated by a Croatian priest sympathetic to his nation's fascist Ustashe movement. Among those who escaped was Klaus Barbie, the "Butcher of Lyon," who headed the Gestapo in France. (Barbie was extradited from Bolivia to France in 1983, and died in prison in 1991.)

As a military lifer, General Franks is probably also familiar with an alternative definition of *ratline*, unique to the Virginia Military Institute. First-year students are subjected to a six-to-seven-month indoctrination program of marching, push-ups, crawls through the mud, and verbal abuse. Because the freshmen are called rats by the upperclassmen tormentors, the regimen is traditionally referred to as the ratline. There is no secret escape; students must endure or drop out.

FOREIGNERS

WHY DOES IT **COST SO MUCH** TO LIVE IN GABON?

WHY DO **BRITISH ROYALS** WEAR MILITARY **UNIFORMS?**

WHAT'S THE **PARIS CLUB?**

WHO RUNS **ANTARCTICA?**

HOW DO **BASQUE** AND **SPANISH** DIFFER?

DOES **IRAN'S** PARLIAMENT HAVE ANY CLOUT?

WHY DO BRITISH ROYALS WEAR MILITARY UNIFORMS?

During the queen mum's funeral in April 2002, many of the British royals donned full military uniforms. Prince Charles wore the dress uniform of a rear admiral, Prince Andrew the uniform of a royal naval commander, and even Princess Anne the trousers of a rear admiral. Why do British royals wear military uniforms?

Frequently, the royals earn their uniforms the hard way. Both Prince Charles and Prince Andrew, for example, had long careers in the military. Prince Andrew retired from active service in 2001 after serving as an officer in the royal navy for over twenty years, earning the title of commander in the process. Prince Charles served as an air vice marshal in the royal air force and rear admiral in the navy, retiring in 1976 after seven years of active service. Other times, royals collect military ranks and uniforms as honorifics. Princess Anne didn't serve in the military, but she can wear military trousers because she is an honorary rear admiral. In addition to his earned military ranks, Prince Charles is the honorary colonel in chief of seventeen regiments of the armed services.

Custom holds that those royals who don't hold a military rank wear standard mourning garb at state funerals. Prince Edward, who served only briefly in the military and holds no important earned or honorary rank, wore a long black morning coat to his grandmother's funeral.

Royals have donned military dress at state occasions since the nineteenth century. Princess Anne's military trousers were a departure from the norm, however. Though the queen mum's funeral marked the second time Princess Anne has made the feminist gesture, she reportedly is the first royal woman to wear military attire in public since Queen Elizabeth I—in 1588. For that occasion, in which the queen rallied British troops at Tilbury to battle the Spanish, she wore a suit of armor.

WHY DOES IT COST SO MUCH TO LIVE IN GABON?

A 2003 report from the Economist Intelligence Unit (EIU) listed Libreville, Gabon, as the world's fourth most expensive city, tied with Hong Kong and ahead of Paris, London, and New York. How did a third world capital get so pricey?

The EIU survey measures the cost of living for an expatriate or foreigner moving into a country—not the native population. (It's designed to assist corporations in budgeting for overseas travel.) So in the case of Libreville, the high price is a result of the short supply of goods and accommodations acceptable to foreigners. For example, unless an expat wishes to live in a Libreville neighborhood where electricity and clean water aren't a sure thing, he or she is forced to huddle in the city's Western-style hotels or villas—and pay a king's ransom for the privilege. Luxuries such as whiskey, tobacco, and grooming products are also tossed into the EIU's equation—luxuries that are primarily purchased by Libreville's foreign-born residents, and for which they are charged a steep out-of-towner's premium.

The expats shrug off the price-gouging because Gabon is sub-Saharan Africa's third leading producer of oil behind Nigeria and Angola. Eighty percent of the nation's exports consist of crude oil, with the United States alone buying $1.6 billion worth of petroleum. The vast majority of visitors to Gabon, then, are employees of energy companies like Shell and Amoco; of the 120,000 foreigners who set foot in Gabon last year, only about 1 percent were tourists. Traveling oilmen, of course, come equipped with healthy expense accounts, and thus don't blanch when served a $15 basket of fries.

The price-gouging isn't totally predatory, especially when it comes to food. The Gabonese government's infatuation with oil production has left the nation's agricultural sector woefully underdeveloped. Only 1 percent of Gabon is under cultivation, and many of those farms are of the subsistence variety. So snagging a meal in Libreville can be a wallet-draining experience—perhaps not on par with a Kobe beef supper in Tokyo, the EIU survey's most expensive city, but close enough to scare away scraggly backpackers. That's terrible news for Gabon's Ministry of Tourism, which is trying to sell the country as an ecotourism paradise. "Beautiful Forests at Hong Kong Prices" just isn't going to cut it as a marketing slogan.

WHAT'S THE PARIS CLUB?

In 2003, the Paris Club, which bills itself as "an informal group of official creditors," studied ways to reduce Iraq's debt load. What's the Paris Club, and who's on the membership list?

The club traces its roots back nearly half a century, to an Argentinean financial crisis during the Peronist unrest of 1956. Teetering on the brink of default, Argentina met with several of its sovereign creditors in Paris to arrange a rescheduling of its debt payments. The negotiations helped stave off economic catastrophe and convinced the creditor nations that with multilateral cooperation they could prevent future third world implosions. By meeting to come up with less onerous payment plans, which would typically include at least partial debt forgiveness, creditor nations could ensure that everyone got paid in a timely fashion. (If only a few creditors played nice, the debtors would have to pay off the less forgiving nations first, and there might be nothing left for the reschedulers.)

Thus was born the Paris Club, which meets every six weeks at France's Ministry of the Economy, Finance, and Industry. The meetings are chaired by a senior official of the French Treasury and attended by financial pooh-bahs from nineteen of the world's wealthiest nations. (The United States sends representatives from the Department of the Treasury.) Behind closed doors, they consider appeals from the desperate, especially countries whose debt quagmires may stem from military conflict or brutal dictatorship. These debtors are often recommended by the International Monetary Fund, and only after they've already tried austerity plans and other reforms. A debt rescheduling or debt cancellation by the Paris Club is often viewed as a last resort before default.

Aside from "an informal group," the club also calls itself a "noninstitution," since its decisions are not legally binding. The club provides the rescheduling framework, but each member is left to negotiate the particulars bilaterally with the debtor in question; the honor system compels the members to abide by the club's terms. One of the core principles of the club is that no creditor can profit from a rescheduling; the terms they reach with Moldova, Nigeria, Mauritania, or other supplicants must involve at least some modicum of financial sacrifice.

Among the club's recent handiwork was a deal in April 2002 to reschedule $5.4 billion worth of Indonesia's debt, and a 2001 decision to reschedule $12.5 billion in Pakistani debt over a 38-year stretch. Also in 2001, the club canceled $3 billion of Yugoslavia's debt, recognizing that nearly a decade's worth of war had sapped the country's ability to pay.

The Paris Club isn't always so accommodating when it comes to dealing with crises. In 1999, a club delegation was sent to Cuba, to stress the group's grave concern over the $11.2 billion tab Fidel Castro had run up. (Cuba's debt, however, was not rescheduled by the club.) And when Russia was late with its rescheduled payments the following year, the club sent a grim note warning of "unfortunate damage to Russia's hopes for improved access to capital markets" should the dithering continue.

Bonus Explainer: There's also a London Club, made up primarily of commercial banks. Founded in the 1970s and modeled on the Paris Club, the British version shoots for the same goal, preferring reduced payments to defaults. The London Club is even more informal than its Gallic elder, however; it meets solely on an ad hoc basis, whenever a debtor country requests relief.

WHO RUNS ANTARCTICA?

In October 1999, an American doctor was evacuated from an Antarctic research station after treating herself for breast cancer for five months. Who lives in Antarctica? What sort of research is done there? And who is in charge?

At 5.5 million square miles, Antarctica is the fifth largest continent (Australia and Europe are smaller), but its forbidding climate has kept the population from exceeding a few thousand. With a mean annual temperature of 70 degrees below zero Fahrenheit and a surface that is 98 percent covered in ice, Antarctica has no indigenous inhabitants and very few native plants and animals. Fossil discoveries suggest that it was part of Gondwanaland, the single temperate continent, 200 million years ago.

Antarctica was unknown to humans until American sealer John Davis made landfall in 1821. For the next hundred years, a dozen countries shared the continent. Some—such as Norway and Sweden—were interested in whaling and fur sealing. Others—Britain and the United States, for example—were primarily concerned with exploration and scientific research. First to reach the South Pole was Norway's Roald Amundsen in 1911. The continent was mapped in the late 1920s, setting off an international land rush.

In 1959, twelve nations including the United States and the Soviet Union signed the Antarctic Treaty. It guarantees cooperation and free movement among scientific operations, prohibits military activities, and suspends indefinitely all territorial claims. Under the treaty, Antarctica is governed through consultative meetings of the nations—now numbering twenty-seven—that maintain extensive Antarctic facilities. Most meetings focus on environmental protections: In 1991, the group banned oil and mineral exploration for the next fifty years. They have also restricted fishing and banned sealing altogether. American laws apply to U.S. nationals in Antarctica, except when they are in foreign-operated research stations.

Since adoption of the treaty, Antarctica has been inhabited exclusively by scientific researchers and support staff. Antarctica is uniquely suited for many types of research, including astronomy, atmospheric science, meteorology, oceanography, and geophysics. There are 80 research stations scattered across Antarctica, only 40 of which are active in the winter. McMurdo station, run by the United States, is the largest, with 80 buildings and 1,000 summer residents. The settlements are isolated during the eight winter months, March through October, when brutal weather makes air travel all but impossible. As a result, few researchers stay in Antarctica for more than one or two years at a time.

HOW DO BASQUE AND SPANISH DIFFER?

The Basque separatist group ETA has been blamed for deadly bombings in Spain. Basque nationalists often cite the group's distinct language as a primary reason for independence. How different is the Basque tongue from Spanish?

Aside from a few similar pronunciation characteristics, like trilled r's, the two are completely unrelated. In fact, Basque—more formally known as Euskara—is one of the planet's most unusual languages. Though linguists have tried to connect Euskara to everything from Pictish to the Dravidian languages, the current consensus is that it is not related to any other. It doesn't seem to belong to the Indo-European language family and likely predates the development of those tongues. One theory, popular among Basque scholars, is that both the language and the ethnic group descend from the Iberian peninsula's earliest settlers, who may have arrived around 35,000 years ago. There is scant archaeological evidence, however, to support this assertion.

What is certain is that an ancestral form of Basque, known as Aquitanian, was being spoken when the Romans arrived in Spain, around 200 B.C. Though the Basques came down from the Pyrenees to trade with the conquerors, they were never thoroughly subjugated, which may account for the perseverance of Euskara while the rest of the peninsula was influenced by Latin. In the Middle Ages, Basque was widely spoken in northeastern Spain and southwestern France. Between 1200 and 1332, the three Basque provinces of Guipuzcoa, Vizcaya, and Alava allied themselves with the Castilian crown, but they were granted special privileges, including self-government.

The first wave of oppression followed the Carlist Wars of the nineteenth century, after the Basques supported the losing cause of the pretender Don Carlos. Things got much worse under Generalissimo Francisco Franco, who came to power after the Spanish Civil War and outlawed the speaking of Euskara. This repression, some claim, led to the creation of ETA (Euskadi Ta Askatasuna—"Basque Homeland and Liberty") in 1959. Though the Basque region was granted considerable autonomy after Franco's death, a small faction of separatists continues to fight for complete independence. There have been more than 800 people killed as a result of ETA attacks since 1968.

There are about 600,000 fluent Euskara speakers in Basque country today, with the vast majority on the Spanish side, and another 400,000 speak some Euskara. There has been a tremendous Euskara revival in Basque schools over the past two decades. A sign of the Basques' pride in their tongue is their word for themselves, Euskaldunak—"possessors of the Basque language."

DOES IRAN'S PARLIAMENT HAVE ANY CLOUT?

In June 2003, several members of the Iranian parliament openly condemned the arrests of hundreds of student protesters, who had been demonstrating against clerical rule. How much clout does Iran's parliament really have, given the country's theocratic reputation?

The parliament and the president, though democratically elected, are far less powerful than Iran's clerical establishment, which is headed by Supreme Leader Ayatollah Ali Khamenei. The 290 seats in the national legislature, known as the Majlis Shura-e-Islami (Islamic Consultative Assembly), are up for grabs every four years. So, too, is the presidency, currently occupied by Mohammad Khatami. The parliament is not a Soviet-style rubber stamp for the clerics, but rather a chamber that originates, debates, and passes the nation's laws.

It is the religious leaders, however, who ultimately decide which parliamentary laws can stand. Khamenei, appointed for life by the Assembly of Experts in 1989, can veto any law he deems un-Islamic. The Guardian Council, appointed by Khamenei to protect the ideals of the Islamic revolution, also has this power. And it is Khamenei, not the parliament or Khatami, who controls Iran's most potent organs of oppression, such as the judiciary, the Revolutionary Guards, and the state-controlled media.

Still, as a republic rather than a monarchy, Iran allows for considerable voter participation. All candidates for public office must first be approved by the Guardian Council, but even so, electoral contests produce frequent surprises, most famously when Khatami won his first term in 1997. His chief rival, speaker of the parliament Ali Akbar Nateq-Nouri, enjoyed the support of the country's religious leaders, as well as the mainstream press; Khatami, a relative unknown who'd headed Iran's National Library, was scarcely considered a dark horse. But the reformer won in a landslide, garnering nearly 70 percent of the vote. A stunning 88 percent of registered voters showed at the polls. Three years later, reformers affiliated with Khatami won the majority of parliamentary seats. And Khatami was reelected in 2001 by a true landslide margin of around 95 percent. His campaign promised a commitment to "independence, freedom, and progress."

Hard-liners allied with Khamenei have made those goals difficult to achieve. Members of parliament are supposedly guaranteed immunity from prosecution for speaking their minds, but that rule hasn't always been observed. A few politicians have been prosecuted over the years for airing allegedly un-Islamic or counterrevolutionary views. In addition, theocratic thugs often harass and threaten reformers and their families. However, compared to many imprisoned journalists and dissidents, these politicians get off pretty easy.

WHERE THINGS COME FROM

WHERE DOES THE WORD
CAKEWALK
COME FROM?

WHERE DO
MARDI GRAS BEADS
COME FROM?

WHERE DOES THE PHRASE
PIE IN THE SKY
COME FROM?

WHERE DO
TAROT CARDS
COME FROM?

WHERE DOES THE PHRASE
BLUE CHIP
COME FROM?

WHERE DOES
KABBALAH
COME FROM?

WHERE DOES THE
GENEVA CONVENTION
COME FROM?

WHERE DOES THE WORD <u>CAKEWALK</u> COME FROM?

Defense Policy Board member Kenneth Adelman took heat during the second Gulf War for predicting a cakewalk for the United States. Where does the term cakewalk *come from, and why is it synonymous with* easy?

The cakewalk was originally a nineteenth-century dance, invented by African-Americans in the antebellum South. It was intended to satirize the stiff ballroom promenades of white plantation owners, who favored the rigidly formal dances of European high society. Cakewalking slaves lampooned these stuffy moves by overaccentuating their high kicks, bows, and imaginary hat doffings, mixing the cartoonish gestures together with traditional African steps. Likely unaware of the dance's roots in derision, plantation owners often invited their slaves to participate in Sunday contests, to determine which dancers were most elegant and inventive. The winners would receive cake slices, a prize that gave birth to the dance's familiar name.

After Emancipation, the contest tradition continued in black communities; the *Oxford English Dictionary* dates the widespread adoption of *cakewalk* to the late 1870s. It was around this time that *cakewalk* came to mean "easy"—not because the dance was particularly simple to do but rather because of its languid pace and association with weekend leisure.

The cakewalk's fame eventually spread northward, and it became a nationwide fad during the 1890s. Legendary performers Charles Johnson and Dora Dean were the dance's great popularizers, and cakewalk contests were a staple of Manhattan nightlife around the turn of century, for whites as well as blacks. Early ragtime songs, with their trademark syncopated beats and brassy sounds, were often known as cakewalk music.

Cakewalk contests also gave rise to two other well-worn clichés: "That takes the cake!" and "piece of cake." The latter phrase, which also means easy, is believed to have first been used in print by humorist Ogden Nash in *The Primrose Path*.

Southern natives, especially those who grew up attending church socials and PTA fund-raisers, often have a very different definition of *cakewalk*. To them, a cakewalk is a contest similar to musical chairs, in which participants walk around a circle marked off with numbers. When the music stops, the contestants freeze and an emcee calls out a number; whoever's physically closest to that numbered slot wins a sugary treat.

WHERE DO MARDI GRAS BEADS COME FROM?

Each year, New Orleans's Mardi Gras revelers spend their pre-Lenten hours downing Hurricanes, gawking at naked flesh, and begging paraders for colored beads with the traditional plea, "Throw me something, mister!" How did the custom of throwing beads begin?

The first recorded instances of Mardi Gras paraders tossing souvenirs to the crowd date back to the 1840s, when revelers costumed as aristocrats threw out baubles and sugar-coated almonds. Other, less savory characters preferred trick to treat and pelted onlookers with an assortment of dirt, flour, and quicklime. The dissemination of handouts—or throws, in Mardi Gras parlance—is widely believed to have derived from festival customs in Renaissance Europe, where pre-Lenten carnivals often involved projectiles (hurled about after village-wide ale-and-mead binges). Some historians theorize that the tradition has roots in a pagan postwinter ritual, during which lucky peasants who'd survived the cold months celebrated by throwing milled grain into the fields—an offering of gratitude to the deity (or deities) who had given them enough food to last.

Glass beads did not become a New Orleans Mardi Gras staple until the 1880s, after Anglo-American krewes had formed to organize the loose-knit festivities. Legend has it that the first parade participant to use beads was a man dressed up as Santa Claus; the ornamental strands were such a hit that other krewes picked up on the ritual. By 1900, when at least 100,000 tourists a year flocked to the Crescent City for Mardi Gras, beaded throws were ubiquitous.

Today's plastic or aluminum beads have earned substantial notoriety for their role in a sexual bartering system; women often bare their breasts for a strand or two. (And for a particularly enticing throw, sometimes go the Full Monty or worse.) Despite claims that this custom dates back decades, a 1996 paper in the academic journal *Social Forces* could trace the beads-for-nudity movement back only to the 1970s.

Bonus Explainer: A krewe known as Zulu has become famous for handing out (not throwing) Mardi Gras coconuts in lieu of beads. The practice ceased briefly in the 1980s, owing to liability concerns—no insurance company would cover Zulu, fearing that an errant coconut might dent a merrymaker's skull. Zulu leaders appealed to the Louisiana state legislature, pointing out that beads and other Mardi Gras trinkets were exempted from liability laws. In 1987, then governor Edwin Edwards signed the "Coconut Bills," adding Zulu's oblong handouts to the list.

WHERE DOES THE PHRASE PIE IN THE SKY COME FROM?

In January 2003, North Korea spurned an American diplomatic overture, deriding it as "pie in the sky." What are the origins of that oft-used idiom for a sham promise?

It's somewhat fitting that an official from North Korea, the most hard-line Communist nation left on the planet, chose a phrase coined by a champion of the American proletariat. *Pie in the sky* comes from an early twentieth-century folk song written by labor activist Joe Hill, aka Joe Hillstrom, a legendary member of the Industrial Workers of the World. The song, entitled "The Preacher and the Slave," is a satiric attack on the Salvation Army, whose preachers Hill decried for lulling workers into complacency. The first verse goes:

You will eat, bye and bye,
In that glorious land above the sky;
Work and pray, live on hay,
You'll get pie in the sky when you die.

"The Preacher and the Slave" was included in the *Little Red Songbook* distributed to IWW members, who were also known as Wobblies. (The nickname's origins are much debated; one possible explanation is that it stems from the flexible wobble saws used to chop down trees.) Other Hill-penned numbers in the motivational songbook included "The Rebel Girl" and "Workers of the World, Awaken!"

A Swedish immigrant born Joel Emmanuel Haggland, Hill is perhaps most famous for the sensational circumstances surrounding his death. He was found guilty of murdering a Salt Lake City shopkeeper in 1914 and executed by firing squad the following year. The Wobblies believed the charges were trumped up as payback for Hill's musical activism.

WHERE DO TAROT CARDS COME FROM?

During their killing spree in 2002, the D.C. snipers left a tarot card inscribed with "Dear Policeman, I am God" near the scene of one shooting. Where do tarot cards come from?

Tarot cards likely originated in northern Italy during the late fourteenth or early fifteenth century. The oldest surviving set, known as the Visconti-Sforza deck, was created for the Duke of Milan's family around 1440. The cards were used to play a bridge-like game known as *tarocchi,* popular at the time among nobles and other leisure lovers. According to tarot historian Gertrude Moakley, the cards' fanciful images—from the Fool to Death—were inspired by the costumed figures who participated in carnival parades.

The game of tarocchi eventually spread to other European

countries, including southern France, where it was renamed tarot. The cards were not regarded as mystical until the late eighteenth century, when the occult came into vogue. A man named Antoine Court de Gébelin wrote a popular book linking the cards to ancient Egyptian lore, arguing that tarot symbols contained the secret wisdom of a god called Thoth. Around the same time, Jean-Baptiste Alliette, writing under the pseudonym Etteilla, published a treatise on using tarot cards as divination tools.

The popularity of tarot cards spread as Europe's fascination with the occult grew. French writer Eliphas Lévi popularized the notion that tarot symbols were somehow connected with the Hebrew alphabet, and thus to the Jewish mystical tradition of kabbalah. A pseudoscholarly book called *The Tarot of the Bohemians* put forth the notion that tarot cards were a Gypsy invention. (At the time, Gypsies were believed to have originated in Egypt, which many nineteenth-century Europeans fancied as the cradle of human knowledge.)

Mystical groups such as the Theosophical Society and the Rosicrucians turned tarot into an American fad during the early 1900s. Many American tarot practitioners use a set of cards known as the Waite-Smith deck, created in 1909 by A. E. Waite, a British member of the Hermetic Order of the Golden Dawn, and the artist Pamela Colman Smith. Another popular deck, the Book of Thoth, was developed by magician-cum-guru Aleister Crowley. Both have become de rigueur accessories for modern fortune-tellers.

WHERE DOES THE GENEVA CONVENTION COME FROM?

Donald Rumsfeld claimed Iraqis violated the Geneva Convention by broadcasting interrogations with captured American soldiers. The document, he pointed out, explicitly forbids the humiliation of prisoners of war. Where did the Geneva Convention come from?

A stickler for legal accuracy would first point out that it should be Geneva Conventions, plural. The treaty that Rumsfeld cites is formally known as the third convention, which deals with the treatment of POWs. The first convention covers the handling of sick and wounded soldiers; the second, injured sailors and shipwreck victims; and the fourth, civilians during wartime. Though the current conventions are not quite fifty-four years old, Geneva-based efforts for more compassionate warfare date back to the mid–nineteenth century. In 1859, a Swiss businessman named Henri Dunant traveled to northern Italy, hoping to gain an audience with French emperor Napoleon III.

According to Caroline Moorehead's 1999 book *Dunant's Dream,* he stumbled upon the Battle of Solferino, a key conflict in Piedmont's war for Italian independence against Austria. Dunant was taken aback by the suffering of the wounded, often left to die in agony amid vermin-infested muck and decaying bodies. The French army, which was fighting alongside the Piedmontese, had only one doctor per 1,000 soldiers.

Dunant rallied local peasants to carry the wounded to nearby churches and to attend to their injuries as best as possible. (However, given the dearth of medicines or physicians, the care usually amounted to little more than a belt of wine and a prayer.) Appalled by the carnage, and influenced by Florence Nightingale's legendary nursing work in the Crimea, Dunant wrote *A Memory of Solferino* in 1862. The pamphlet introduced the notion of an independent organization that would tend to wartime casualties—the International Committee of the Red Cross (ICRC), which was officially created a year later.

Yet Dunant feared that, without official international recognition, ICRC medics might be harmed as they performed their duties. So, in 1864, he convinced the Swiss government to hold a sixteen-nation conference, which produced the ten-article Geneva Convention for the Amelioration of the Condition of the Wounded in Armies in the Field. The treaty, often regarded as the first example of international humanitarian law, was instantly ratified by twelve of the attendees; the United States held out until 1882. The initial convention was tweaked slightly in 1906 and then expanded in 1929 to cover the treatment of POWs. The atrocities of World War II, however, led to the wholesale overhaul of the documents in 1949, when the current four conventions were adopted. There were two additional protocols added in 1977 that extend protections to victims of nontraditional conflicts: wars of self-determination and civil wars.

Those who violate the Geneva Conventions, such as the stipulation in Article 13 of the third convention that POWs must be protected against "insults and public curiosity," risk being tried as war criminals at the International Criminal Court. The ICRC, hoping to give the conventions some teeth, was a prime proponent of the court's creation.

WHERE DOES THE PHRASE <u>BLUE CHIP</u> COME FROM?

The Canadian panic over mad cow disease in May 2003 was a Wall Street bummer for McDonald's, whose stock price slipped 5 percent in a single day. The slide dragged down the Dow Jones industrial average, which included the Golden Arches and twenty-nine other blue chip stocks. Where does the phrase blue chip *come from?*

As befits the high-risk nature of stock picking, *blue chip* derives from poker. The simplest sets of poker betting disks include white, red, and blue chips, with tradition dictating that the blues are highest in value. If a white chip is worth $1, a red is usually worth $5, and a blue $10. No one's quite sure why blue chips were accorded such exalted status, but it may have something to do with the color's royal lineage—an aristocrat, after all, is known as a blue blood. And the wearing of blue-dyed cloth was a privilege of ancient and medieval kings.

Since established blue chip stocks are considered relatively valuable, not to mention pricey, the phrase is appropriate. Most etymologists believe it was first used around 1900, perhaps in 1904, the year the Dow industrial average first broke 100. (That year's Dow included such bygone companies as American Smelting & Refining, Colorado Fuel & Iron, and U.S. Leather.) A few sources date the usage to the 1920s, but this seems dubious. The popularity of poker during Prohibition, and an attendant upswing in the amounts being wagered, led to the manufacture of a rainbow of new betting disks, all ostensibly of higher value than the old blues. One common color scheme from this era fixed black as the highest-value chip, while others employed brown as the Mother of All Chips. Had Wall Street slang-talkers affixed the term during the Hoover years, then, we'd likely be talking about brown chip stocks nowadays.

Bonus Explainer: The hierarchy of colored chips is also much discussed among devotees of Alcoholics Anonymous. Newly recovering alcoholics are rewarded with chips for each month of sobriety, typically starting with a white chip when they begin attending meetings. Practices vary widely from chapter to chapter, but a blue chip is often used to mark two months of sobriety; a clear, silver, or golden chip is a traditional gift for the one-year anniversary.

WHERE DOES KABBALAH COME FROM?

In May 2003, news broke that Madonna spent over $5 million for a London town house that would become a new center for the study of kabbalah. This religious movement, long associated with Judaism, was little known until it became popular among celebrities. What is kabbalah and where does it come from?

The term *kabbalah* comes from the Hebrew word meaning "tradition" or "received knowledge." Kabbalists claim their beliefs date back to the origins of the Torah; the written tradition of God's word, they say, was always accompanied by an oral tradition, or kabbalah, of equal sanctity. This oral tradition contended that God is perceivable as ten different potencies or forms of light (known collectively as the sefirot). Because each one of the ten sefirot has Hebrew characters associated with it, the kabbalah provides a method for interpreting the hidden meanings of the scriptures, and kabbalism aims primarily to decrypt the Torah using these keys. Kabbalists believe the Torah is God itself, and that an infinite store of wisdom can be uncovered by dint of scholarly research.

Kabbalists have been an accepted part of Jewish culture since the twelfth century. Though their mystical beliefs, which focused on the individual's direct communion with God through solitary study, sometimes set them apart from their mainstream coreligionists, many kabbalists were teachers and judges highly respected by all Jews. The emphasis on secret knowledge and mysticism has also long endeared the study of kabbalah to occultists of other persuasions, kicking off a kabbalist fad among gentiles in Renaissance Europe—and giving us words like *cabal*.

In the United States, kabbalism made a comeback in the sixties, when it was championed by Philip Berg, an American former rabbi who began studying kabbalah on a visit to Israel in 1962. Under Berg's leadership, kabbalah in America has greatly expanded, spawning centers around the country and recruiting celebrities such as Madonna and Monica Lewinsky. Berg's version of kabbalah dispenses with the traditional requirements of an Orthodox lifestyle and the study of ancient texts. Where traditional kabbalah emphasizes mysticism as a part of devoted Judaism, Berg's new movement focuses on personal improvement and spiritual happiness, targeted to "people of all faiths and no faiths." Berg's centers draw big crowds for meditation, classes, and philosophical study, and his kabbalah portal offers Kabbalah 101, a class that takes the "once arcane wisdom of Kabbalah and offers it up as [a] user friendly, accessible, self-study program," for $19.95.

How does this new kabbalah stack up against the old? Like traditionalists, Berg presents kabbalah as a way to perceive the inherent order of the universe, the "unseen spiritual laws that govern our lives." The difference is that he simplifies these lessons to make them easily accessible; rather than requiring devotees to learn Hebrew, he publicizes his interpretations of ancient kabbalist texts nationally in books and speaking engagements. Scholars of the field are careful not to slam the new centers too hard, but the experts do argue that Madonna's New Age spiritualism has little in common with the traditional scholarly mysticism of Jewish kabbalah.

WHERE THINGS GO

WHAT HAPPENS TO
**RECALLED
MEAT?**

WHAT HAPPENS TO
**CONFISCATED
NAIL
CLIPPERS?**

WHAT HAPPENS TO
**FROZEN
ASSETS?**

WHAT—AND WHERE—IS THE
STRATEGIC
PETROLEUM RESERVE?

WHAT HAPPENS TO YOUR
**SOCIAL
SECURITY**
NUMBER WHEN YOU DIE?

WHO RECALLS
**ROLLOVER-PRONE
CARS?**

WHAT HAPPENS TO RECALLED MEAT?

Wampler Foods, a division of poultry titan Pilgrim's Pride, recalled 27.4 million pounds worth of cooked deli products in October 2002, fearing it might be contaminated with the potentially lethal bacteria Listeria monocytogenes. *What happens to recalled meat?*

Once consumers return their suspect victuals to the supermarket, the processed turkey and chicken products are usually shipped back to the factory that produced the shady meat. The packages are then sprayed with green dye to make clear that their contents should never be consumed. The meat is then either carted off to landfills, tossed into incinerators, or set aside for rendering into nonhuman protein sources—i.e., dog and livestock food. Listeria, which is frequently present in animal placentas, can be destroyed by subjecting it to temperatures in excess of 160 degrees Fahrenheit, so a long spell of industrial-strength cooking can make recalled turkey pastrami and chicken breasts safe for nonhuman consumption. (However, due in large part to the furor over mad cow disease, there are growing concerns over the wisdom of feeding tainted meat to cattle, regardless of how well it's been heated.)

Some stores may elect to destroy tainted meat on the premises instead of holding it for the trucks, but they need an okay from federal food safety inspectors, who will monitor the disposal process. Given the nastiness of diseases like listeriosis, which is often fatal to infants, the elderly, and others with weakened immune systems, inspectors monitor such recalls very carefully.

WHAT HAPPENS TO CONFISCATED NAIL CLIPPERS?

After September 11, thousands of personal items were seized by airport security: nail clippers, knives, scissors, corkscrews, and so forth. What happens to these confiscated items?

Most of them are thrown away or destroyed. The exact procedure for dealing with confiscated items varies from airport to airport. But the result is usually the same. The items end up in an oven, in an industrial grinder, or in the trash.

There are a lot of items to destroy (or to hand out as bonuses to disgruntled employees): In October 2001, the *Tampa Tribune* reported that 8,626 items had been seized from the Tampa airport since the September 11 terror attacks. Some items on the list: 42 cans of Mace, more than 600 knives, a scalpel, more than 260 corkscrews, 7 rounds of ammunition, 2 spoons, a jar of rubber cement, 3 candles, 6 batteries, 993 pairs of tweezers, and 2,137 pairs of scissors. As a comparison, screeners confiscated 41 items in September 2000.

Occasionally, passengers will protest that certain items are of tangible or sentimental value. In those cases, the best procedure is for passengers to pack the item with their checked luggage. If time is running short, passengers may be able to convince security to send the item to the airport's lost and found. After that, good luck. The Federal Aviation Administration doesn't have a policy about what's done with confiscated personal items. FAA policy is simply that the items can't be brought onto an airplane.

WHAT HAPPENS TO YOUR SOCIAL SECURITY NUMBER WHEN YOU DIE?

In April 2003, the very much alive Jim Pierce was declared dead when a Social Security Administration (SSA) clerk mistakenly typed his Social Security number into a database of the departed.

Are Social Security numbers ever reused once the bearer dies, and how are they generated in the first place?

The SSA is adamant that numbers are never recycled and likely won't be for the foreseeable future. Given the nine-digit format, there are a hair under 1 billion possible permutations, taking into account that numbers like 000-00-0000 and other oddities aren't distributed. So far, the SSA has doled out roughly 400 million numbers. Population researchers calculate that roughly 300 million people will require new Social Security numbers by the year 2050—about 230 million native births plus 68 million immigrants, give or take 50 million all told. Barring unforeseen circumstances, such as a meteor strike or cloning boom, the current enumeration system should last nearly another century.

The numbers of the deceased are made publicly available via the Social Security Death Index. Several genealogy services provide free, searchable versions of the SSDI to aid researchers who are tracing their family roots. Hospitals make it easy for new parents to obtain Social Security numbers for their infants at birth, often integrating the application forms into the standard procedural paperwork. Naturalized citizens and legal aliens can apply directly to the SSA once they are in the United States or as part of the visa application process before they arrive. Paranoid antigovernment types aren't technically required to have a Social Security number, but life in the United States is virtually impossible without one. The IRS requires all employed citizens over 18 to have a number, and a Social Security number is essential to opening up a bank account, paying taxes, and obtaining health insurance. Once you have a number, you can't opt out of the program. On extremely rare occasions you can change your number, but only if you can prove that keeping your current digits is a threat to your well-being—say, if you're being pursued by a relentless stalker.

Conspiracy theories abound as to the significance of the numbers, but the true explanation is mundane. The first three digits are assigned by geographical region. Originally, this was done by state, with the lowest numbers on the Eastern Seaboard and the highest along the Pacific; they are now assigned according to ZIP code. The middle two digits are referred to as the "group number," which simply breaks down each geographic unit into smaller, random subsets—that is, your neighbor's baby may share the same first three digits with your toddler, but the kids' group numbers will likely be different. The last four digits, the serial number, are assigned in chronological order within each area and group number as the applications are processed. Serial number 0000 is never used.

Contrary to the rumors favored by the black-helicopter set, the numbers have nothing to do with racial categorizations or UN relocation plans.

WHAT—AND WHERE—IS THE STRATEGIC PETROLEUM RESERVE?

In December 2002, political tumult in Venezuela had President Bush pondering whether to tap into our nation's Strategic Petroleum Reserve (SPR), which houses around 560 million barrels of crude. Where's all that black gold stored, and what will it take to turn on the spigots?

The SPR is stockpiled at four locations around the Gulf of Mexico, all within shouting distance of major refineries: Bryan Mound and Bill Hill in Texas, and West Hackberry and Bayou Choctaw in neighboring Louisiana. The oil is kept in subterranean salt caverns, where the temperature's just right to maintain the perfect amount of viscosity, and the air pressure prevents the creation of fissures that could cause leakage. It's also cheaper by about a factor of 10 than using aboveground storage tanks. And of course, a salt cavern 2,000 feet below the earth's surface is a target harder for terrorists to attack.

The SPR was created in 1975 as part of the Energy Policy and Conservation Act, largely in response to the OPEC oil embargo of 1973–74. Much of the present-day stockpile is given to the government by companies who prospect for petroleum on federal land as a royalty in lieu of cash. Should things get hairy, energywise, due to international conflict or some other catastrophe, the president alone has the authority to order a drawdown of the reserve, at an estimated rate of 4.1 million barrels per day. Once the president gives the go-ahead order, though, it would take at least fifteen days for the SPR crude to hit the market.

The last significant dip into the SPR occurred during Desert Storm, when Bush the Elder ordered a drawdown of 34 million barrels. There have been minor dips into the kitty since then, such as in June of 2000, when the SPR "lent" 500,000 barrels each to CITGO and Conoco, which were having problems with their tanker fleets. Later that same year, the SPR made 2.8 million barrels of crude available in anticipation of a harsh Northeast winter.

Bonus Explainer: Not all SPR oil is created equal. About a third of the stockpile qualifies as sweet crude, meaning that its sulfur content is less than half of 1 percent. The rest is more sulfur-laden sour crude. Sweet crude is more desirable among refinery pooh-bahs, but when we're in a bind that might require tapping the SPR, beggars can't be choosers.

WHAT HAPPENS TO FROZEN ASSETS?

In December 2001, the Bush administration froze the financial assets of three organizations it accused of having ties to Hamas. What happens to frozen assets?

Nothing, usually. They're held by the banks that had the assets when they were frozen, until they're unfrozen. The U.S. government does not take possession. The Treasury Department's Office of Foreign Assets Control has frozen nearly $4 billion in assets from countries designated as terrorist states by the State Department, including $254 million in Taliban assets in the United States that were frozen in 1999.

Some members of Congress and lawyers want that pot of money to be used to compensate the victims of terrorist attacks. The State Department, however, opposes that idea, believing that it can use the frozen assets as leverage to get states to stop sponsoring terrorism and to become more democratic. The State Department also believes that using frozen assets to pay victims who bring private lawsuits against countries sponsoring terrorism would be unfair to victims of terrorism who don't file lawsuits.

So far, victims have been paid in only a few cases involving Cuba and Iran. Last year, Congress passed a law that led to $97 million being paid from Cuba's frozen assets to the families of the Cuban-American pilots shot down in 1996 by the Cuban government. And the U.S. government paid more than $213 million to eight families who had won judgments against Iran. In exchange, the families dropped their claims against Iran's frozen assets held by the United States. The government hopes to collect from Iran using an international tribunal that was established in 1981 to settle billions of dollars in claims after the Iranian hostage crisis.

WHO RECALLS ROLLOVER-PRONE CARS?

In July 2003, the National Highway Traffic Safety Administration (NHTSA) released its latest rollover resistance ratings, rankings that measure the likelihood that a vehicle will flip onto its roof in the event of an accident. The 2003 Toyota Tacoma Extended Cab 4x4 Pickup received the lowest rating, a mere two stars out of a possible five. How unsafe does a car have to be for the government to demand a recall?

According to the Motor Vehicle Safety Act of 1966, the NHTSA can open a recall investigation only when there's a safety-related defect that can cause death or injury—for example, those infamous Firestone tires—or when a vehicle does not meet the agency's standards. Despite the Tacoma's meager two-star rating, which means it has a 30 percent to 40 percent chance of rolling over should a crash occur, the car has not been found to have any specific defects. And there are currently no federal regulations that mandate a minimum rollover resistance score. (A Toyota spokesman told *The New York Times* that safety improvements were forthcoming in the 2004 model.)

But the mounting number of rollover-related deaths—over 10,000 a year, compared with just 4,000 in 1989—has spurred some legislative action. Last month, the Senate Commerce Committee approved a bill that would require the NHTSA to issue rules that would alleviate the lethality of rollover accidents, most likely by toughening requirements on roof strength.

The bill follows the TREAD Act of 2000, which required the NHTSA to come up with real-world rollover tests. The current rating system relies exclusively on a mathematical formula that factors together a vehicle's width, height, and center of gravity to determine the likelihood of rollover. Later this year, though, the agency will begin conducting tests with crash-test dummies in which the vehicles will be programmed to make indelicate maneuvers known as J-turns and fishhooks. The tests are designed to give the NHTSA a better sense of how to prevent rollover and how to protect those unfortunate drivers who find themselves upside down.

Bonus Explainer: The majority of recalls are voluntary, rather than compelled by the NHTSA. In 2001, for example, of the 14.5 million vehicles that went back to the manufacturer, an estimated 11 million were recalled voluntarily.

 WAR

WHY DO **SURRENDERING SOLDIERS** WAVE WHITE FLAGS?

WHY DO **AMERICAN SOLDIERS** WEAR THE FLAG BACKWARD?

WHO BURIES **DEAD ENEMY** SOLDIERS?

HOW DO THE **PENTAGON'S** WAR GAMES WORK?

WHY DID TROOPS WEAR **DARK-GREEN CAMO** IN THE DESERT?

WHAT ARE THE **RULES** OF WAR?

WHY DO SURRENDERING SOLDIERS WAVE WHITE FLAGS?

During the second Gulf War, hundreds of Iraqi soldiers surrendered by waving white flags, the international symbol of capitulation. How did this tradition originate?

Ancient historians from both China and Rome noted the use of white flags to signal surrender. In the former empire, the tradition is believed to have originated with the reign of the Eastern Han dynasty (A.D 25–220), though it may be somewhat older. The Roman writer Cornelius Tacitus mentions a white flag of surrender in his *Histories,* first published in A.D. 109. His reference concerns the Second Battle of Cremona, fought between the Vitellians and the Vespasians in A.D. 69; at the time, the more common Roman token of surrender was for soldiers to hold their shields above their heads. It is believed that the tradition developed independently in the East and West.

As for the selection of such a bland color, it was likely just a matter of convenience in the ancient world. Artificial colors were still centuries away, so white clothes were always handy—not to mention highly visible against most natural backgrounds. Vexillologists (those who study flags) also opine that plain white provided an obvious contrast to the colorful banners that armies often carried into battle.

The peacemaking symbolism of the white flag is now enshrined in the Geneva Conventions, though it's rarely mentioned in national flag codes. Italy is perhaps the only country whose flag guidelines specifically mention the white flag as an indication that a fighting force wants to call for a parley or surrender negotiations.

Iraqi soldiers were well aware that simply waving a white

handkerchief could save their necks. So, too, were their commanders. In the first Gulf War, many Iraqi army officers forced their conscripts to hand over any and all articles of white clothing, including undershirts and socks, lest they be tempted to surrender to American forces. Fortunately for the troops, putting one's hands above one's head is often an equally effective way to cry uncle.

Bonus Explainer: In the latter part of the Civil War, the Confederacy adopted a new national flag known as the Stainless Banner. The flag was predominantly white, with the familiar stars-and-bars design tucked into the upper left-hand corner. Confederate naval commanders detested the flag, as it was often mistaken as a sign of surrender when flying from their masts. About a month before Appomattox, the Confederate Congress added a red bar to the banner's right-hand side, to reduce the confusion.

WHO BURIES DEAD ENEMY SOLDIERS?

During the second Gulf War, cable-news viewers grew accustomed to the grisly sight of dead Iraqi troops. Do passing U.S. forces stop to bury the enemy's dead, or do they leave the remains alone?

Military regulations stipulate that "Army units will be required to bury enemy soldiers as time permits." Given the haste with which frontline troops must move, however, the somber task is often left up to support units, who sweep in after the heaviest combat has died down. The chief mission for so-called graves-registration units is to collect the American dead so the remains can be shipped back to the United States for proper burial. Their secondary duty is to see that enemy casualties are buried with respect, in accordance with the Geneva Conventions' protocols on the handling of remains. Since the Iraqi military apparently had scant resources available to dedicate to the undertaking, the job was mostly left up to the United States.

American soldiers charged with burying Iraqis would first

search the bodies for dangerous items, such as grenades or other explosive ordnance. If the deceased was carrying any sort of personal identification, such as a dog tag or an ID card, that information was recorded and relayed back to mortuary affairs staff in Kuwait. When the war ended, these people were able to locate and notify the next of kin, or at least answer questions if a grieving relative inquired. The remains were then placed in black body bags and laid to rest in simple graves dug out with backhoes. Metal posts were used in lieu of headstones.

On occasion, when they have a respite from battle, frontline units will take on burials themselves, provided they have the heavy equipment necessary to dig sufficiently deep trenches. These troops may lack body bags, in which case the enemies are buried without. Still, markers are always left, and identification details are recorded. The idea is that rapid burial, however unadorned, is preferable to letting the remains be picked apart by wild dogs and other scavengers.

American troops did their best to bury Iraqi troops in accordance with Muslim tradition—with bodies interred to point toward Mecca, for example—but the rituals can't be perfect. Graves-registration units often feature female soldiers, and Muslim custom forbids women from handling male remains.

WHY DO AMERICAN SOLDIERS WEAR THE FLAG BACKWARD?

Many sharp-eyed civilians have noted an apparent oddity on the uniform sleeves of American soldiers: backward flag patches. Why is Old Glory flipped around like that?

Only the flag patches affixed to right shoulders of uniforms are reversed, so the blue field of stars faces forward. (Left shoulder patches aren't a problem, as the stars face forward without meddling.) The reversal is inspired by the age-old practice of carrying flags into battle. When fastened to a standard, the American flag's blue-and-white portion is always closest to the pole. A flag bearer rushing into the fray, then, would naturally lead with the stars. In fact, it would be virtually impossible to lead with the stripes—the flag would simply wilt and wrap around the pole, rather than waving triumphantly in the wind.

For a soldier to lead with shoulder-borne stripes, then, might smack of cowardice and retreat, as if the toter were backpedaling away from the conflict. The official Army guidelines on the donning of flag patches add that the forward-facing stars give "the effect of the flag flying in the breeze as the wearer moves forward." So perhaps it's best to think of every soldier as a latter-day flag bearer, leading the headlong charge into battle.

It should also be noted that military flag patches are often trimmed with gold borders. This is in imitation of the gold-fringed flag, also known as the U.S. military flag. According to an executive order signed by President Dwight D. Eisenhower in 1959, the gold-fringed flag (and, by extension, patch-sized replicas) are to be used exclusively by the armed forces. That order isn't always obeyed, however; many federal courtrooms now feature gold-fringed flags, despite the fact that they should appear only during courts-martial.

HOW DO THE PENTAGON'S WAR GAMES WORK?

In August 2002, the United States military completed its biggest war game to date, a three-week-long, $235 million exercise called Millennium Challenge. How do modern war games work?

Every good war game starts with a plausible scenario. In the case of Millennium Challenge 2002, the U.S. military (known as the Blue force) was pitted against a Persian Gulf nation controlled by a megalomaniac dictator (no, not Iraq, but the Red force). Specifics of the scenario are classified, but the game is widely believed to have centered on a mock invasion of the Red force's territory.

There are two components to a war game: field exercises and

command post exercises. For the former, actual troops are dispatched to either defend or attack mock airfields, communications centers, and other militarily significant sites. Millennium Challenge 2002 involved nine such sites in California and Nevada, two states whose climate and terrain closely mimic those of the Near East. Hundreds of paratroopers from the 82nd Airborne, for example, were dispatched to capture a Red airfield in the Mojave Desert. Once secured, the airfield served as a staging ground for C-130 cargo planes to deliver Stryker armored vehicles, which then attacked adjacent facilities acting as chemical weapons plants. Live ammunition was verboten—electronic sensors mounted on people, vehicles, and buildings tallied the damage.

Command post exercises, by contrast, are exclusively virtual affairs. Generals, colonels, and other high-ranking officers sit in command centers and move around blue or red dots on screens, not terribly unlike Matthew Broderick playing Global Thermonuclear War in the 1983 film *WarGames*. Such exercises are good approximations of large-scale maneuvers, which cannot be easily replicated in the real world. It's one thing to stage a small airfield seizure, quite another to float an aircraft carrier group into a waterway that accurately approximates the Persian Gulf.

Many war games are scripted—that is, both Red and Blue officers are required to perform certain attacks and responses. A smaller number are free play, which means anything goes. Controversy erupted over Millennium Challenge 2002 when the Red forces, commanded by a retired Marine general named Paul Van Riper, engaged in some clever free play tricks that deviated from what the Blues were expecting. Van Riper used virtual motorcycle messengers to relay orders to his virtual field commanders, for example, thereby negating the Americans'—er, Blue force's— ability to eavesdrop. Mere days into the game, a squad of Red digital soldiers had sunk several Blue ships in the Persian Gulf by carrying out suicide attacks with explosives-laden speedboats. That's not in the script, countered the referees, who ordered the Blue fleet to be magically resurrected.

WHY DID TROOPS WEAR DARK-GREEN CAMO IN THE DESERT?

Despite the desert conditions of the recent Iraqi campaign, many American soldiers sported deep-green combat fatigues. Why did troops don woodland camouflage?

According to published reports, the Pentagon simply goofed by not anticipating the demand for sand-colored desert fatigues, formally known as battle-dress uniforms (BDUs). When Army and Marine units were preparing for deployment, several discovered that they lacked enough desert BDUs to outfit each soldier with the requisite three outfits. The UPI reported that the Army's Fourth Infantry Division, headquartered at Fort Hood, Texas, chose to dress all its troops in the more traditional green fatigues—commonly referred to as woodland BDUs—rather than have only some don desert dress. Homogeneity is generally preferred among military commanders.

Units that departed for the Middle East in early 2003 were promised fresh BDUs upon arrival, but shipments were slow to arrive; support commanders reported in March that they had already run out of desert fatigues. The Pentagon's Defense Supply Center in Philadelphia ordered manufacturers to increase production of desert camouflage at the expense of woodland BDUs.

A dearth of appropriately stealthy uniforms was also a problem during the first Gulf War, as many U.S. troops were forced to wear dark green. The Pentagon learned at least one lesson from the 1991 conflict, however: The Marines' anti-chemical-weapons suits, known as mission-oriented protective posture (MOPP) clothing, used to be available only in woodland patterns. The latest MOPP gear features a three-color desert design.

Military leaders insisted that the shortage of desert BDUs would not affect the safety of American soldiers. They pointed out that Iraq's terrain is not entirely Sahara-like, and that green camouflage may have actually been ideal near the banks of the Euphrates River, where vegetation and mud are present.

Bonus Explainer: The Pentagon is not alone in its camouflage foibles. The Canadian military was heavily criticized for dispatching troops to Afghanistan in woodland dress during Operation Enduring Freedom. In March 2003, Canada's red-faced Defence Department officially put a rush on an order for desert BDUs, which were to be sent to the 2,000 peacekeepers the country had committed to Afghanistan.

WHAT ARE THE RULES OF WAR?

In a New York Times *article about a deadly raid he led while in Vietnam, former senator Bob Kerrey said that during a visit to West Point in 2001 he read the rules of war for the first time. What are the rules of war?*

U.S. military personnel are governed by two sets of guidelines on how to behave during war or lesser conflicts. One is codified in the Army field manual *The Law of Land Warfare,* first published in 1956, which draws on international law, such as the Geneva Conventions. The manual's basic principle is that military personnel should "refrain from employing any kind or degree of violence which is not actually necessary for military purposes and that they conduct hostilities with regard for the principles of humanity and chivalry." More specifically, it describes such things as the protection of civilians and the sick and wounded from combat, the proper treatment of prisoners of war, and restrictions on certain types of weapons.

The second set of guidelines, subsidiary to the first, is known as the rules of engagement. The rules of engagement are specific to each military situation and can be modified as circumstances change. For example, the rules of engagement might state that soldiers cannot fire on suspected enemy positions without positive identification of the enemy (being fired upon is always considered positive identification). Or that a U.S. airplane cannot fire on another aircraft simply because the other craft buzzed it but must wait for a more overtly hostile action. Of course, none of the laws and rules is meant to undermine the ultimate right of self-defense.

During Vietnam military personnel were given at best cursory lessons about the laws of warfare; today everyone in the armed forces is required to attend a yearly class on the subject. And the whole notion of rules of engagement was far more lax during Vietnam than it is now. Today, for example, soldiers get more than just verbal instructions; they might also be issued cards with written instructions on the current rules of engagement of their particular mission.

KNOW YOUR RIGHTS

WHY CAN **SHOPPING MALLS** LIMIT FREE **SPEECH?**

DO YOU OWN THE **MOVIE RIGHTS** TO YOUR LIFE?

DOES YOUR **SPIT HAVE** FIFTH AMENDMENT RIGHTS?

WHAT IF YOUR LAWYER **ISN'T REALLY** A LAWYER?

IS A **CANADIAN SAME-SEX** MARRIAGE VALID IN THE UNITED STATES?

DO **DEAD AUTHORS** HOLD ON TO THEIR **COPYRIGHTS?**

DO YOU OWN THE MOVIE RIGHTS TO YOUR LIFE?

In spring 2003, NBC announced plans to make a movie about Private First Class Jessica Lynch, the rescued American POW, even if it didn't get her permission. Can the network do that? Doesn't NBC need to buy the movie rights to her life?

Yes, it can, and no, it doesn't—so long as NBC sticks to the facts.

People don't own movie rights to their lives. Facts, even facts about particular people, are not exclusively owned by anyone. That's why newspapers may write about people without their permission, and why biographers may create unauthorized biographies. The term *movie rights* originally comes from copyright law, under which authors own the exclusive rights to authorize movies based on their works of fiction. But copyright law protects only creative expression, not facts.

The so-called right of publicity does give people a limited right to control commercial use of their names, likenesses, and identities. But the right doesn't extend to news reporting, biography, fiction, and most entertainment, or to the advertising of such works. Generally, the right of publicity applies only to commercial advertising of other products and to merchandising. So NBC could make a movie about Lynch without her permission, but it probably couldn't sell Jessica Lynch action figures.

Likewise, the so-called disclosure of private facts tort (which is one of the several different legal theories that sometimes go by the label *right of privacy*) lets people block publication of certain highly intimate facts about themselves. But this tort has been defined quite narrowly—largely for First Amendment reasons—and doesn't apply to any facts that courts conclude are newsworthy. So even fairly private details of Lynch's captivity likely would be legal for NBC to report. That holds true even if Lynch is found to be a private figure rather than a public figure. The law recognizes that newsworthy events can happen even to private figures, and that those events may legally be reported (or used as the basis for TV movies).

Why then do we often hear of studios buying movie rights to people's lives? One reason is to get the subject's cooperation. Lynch doubtless knows lots of things about her captivity that others don't know (or aren't telling). So the NBC people might make a better movie if Lynch and her family were talking to them. NBC might also want to get Lynch to promise not to talk to any other networks so that it can hawk its movie as an exclusive.

A second reason is that Lynch might be able to sue if NBC gets some facts wrong. If an error in the TV movie injures her reputation, she could sue for defamation; but even if the false claims reflect well on her, she might still be able to sue NBC for placing her in a false light, so long as the error would be something that a reasonable person would find highly offensive. (For instance, if NBC exaggerates Lynch's heroism, she might be able to sue on the grounds that a reasonable person would find it highly offensive to get credit for heroic acts she didn't commit.) And it's quite possible that NBC will get some facts wrong. For instance, since the network doesn't know just how Lynch interacted with her captors, any dialogue or action they include in those scenes will necessarily be fictionalized, possibly to a substantial degree. By getting Lynch's cooperation, NBC could also get her to promise not to sue even if there are some inaccuracies. In this sense, movie rights really means the right to make mistakes.

Finally, a third reason: Though the rules Explainer describes are pretty well established, their precise boundaries aren't always completely clear, which leaves room for (expensive) legal debate. Studios may therefore sometimes pay off the subject to prevent the risk of a lawsuit that—even if it ultimately loses—could possibly delay a multimillion-dollar production.

WHY CAN SHOPPING MALLS LIMIT FREE SPEECH?

*In March 2003, 61-year-old Stephen Downs was arrested for refus-
ing to remove a T-shirt with the words "Peace on Earth" and "Give
Peace a Chance" in a shopping mall in Albany, New York. Why don't
citizens have the same free speech rights in shopping centers that
they do on city streets and parks?*

Because malls are private property, and our constitutional rights are
triggered only when the government (and not a private citizen) tries
to limit our freedoms. As malls expand to include outdoor boule-
vards, movie theaters, and coffeehouses, many contend that we
should have the right of free expression in these private forums.
They argue that malls play the same role that city streets and town
squares once played in our democracy. The first cases asserting the
rights of free speech in privately owned shopping centers were
successful. In the 1946 case of *Marsh v. Alabama,* the Supreme
Court held that the business district of a privately owned company
town was the same as a public street for First Amendment purposes, finding that "the more an owner, for his advantage, opens
up his property for use by the public in general, the more do his
rights become circumscribed by the statutory and constitutional
rights of those who use it." A 1968 case—*Amalgamated Food
Employees Union v. Logan Valley Plaza*—held that a privately owned
mall was the "functional equivalent" of the business district in
Marsh.

But realizing they had overreached in the early cases, and sensitive to what they had done to private property rights, the
Supremes reversed course in *Hudgens v. NLRB,* a 1976 case holding that the First Amendment guarantees no free speech rights in
private shopping centers. And in an important 1980 case, *Pruneyard v. Robins,* the court upheld the general notion that citizens
have no First Amendment rights to express themselves in privately owned shopping centers while still agreeing that a group of
California students had the right to hand out leaflets and collect
signatures in a private California mall.

The magic bullet in *Pruneyard?* The high court found that state constitutions may confer upon citizens broader speech rights than the federal Constitution, and the broadly worded California constitution gave citizens the right to speak freely, even in private malls. The court dismissed the shopping center's claims that such a rule infringed on *its* free speech rights by forcing it to tolerate unwanted speech on private property, and rejected the argument that forcing the shopping center to open up to public debate constituted an unconstitutional taking of private property.

Pruneyard was an invitation from the high court to the states to amend and interpret their own state constitutions so as to permit free speech in private forums if they desired to do so. But twenty-three years later, only six states have joined California in recognizing a state constitutional right to speak and assemble on private property: New Jersey, Colorado, Oregon, Massachusetts, Washington, and Pennsylvania (and several of them have waffled after doing so). Even the states conferring these broader speech rights do so on only two types of private property—shopping malls and nonpublic universities—and the only speech protected there is political speech.

The New York Court of Appeals expressly refused to apply New York's constitutional protections to free speech in shopping malls, which is why Stephen Downs was hauled away for suggesting that we give peace a chance. The charges were later dropped.

DOES YOUR SPIT HAVE FIFTH AMENDMENT RIGHTS?

Virginia's legislature passed a law in February 2002 that allows the state to take a DNA sample from anyone arrested for a violent felony. If the Fifth Amendment protects us from self-incrimination, how can people be forced into providing evidence such as DNA samples or bodily fluids against their will?

The self-incrimination clause of the Fifth Amendment reads that no "person . . . shall be compelled in any criminal case to be a witness against himself." But the courts have long interpreted this narrowly to mean that the Fifth Amendment protects suspects only from being forced to produce "testimonial or communicative" evidence. The Fifth Amendment does not protect suspects from being compelled to produce "real or physical evidence." As Oliver Wendell Holmes once wrote, "the prohibition of compelling a man in a criminal court to be witness against himself is a prohibition of the use of physical or moral compulsion to extort communications from him, not an exclusion of his body as evidence when it may be material."

This distinction between testimonial or communicative evidence and nontestimonial (real or physical) evidence means that the Fifth Amendment does not protect you from being forced to submit to such things as fingerprinting, photographing, measurements, blood samples, or DNA evidence. Nor does it protect you against standing in a lineup or demonstrating your walk.

The Fifth Amendment doesn't even mean that you can't be forced to speak. The Supreme Court has held that the state can force a suspect to speak if it's for the purpose of identifying the physical properties of his or her voice and not for providing testimony.

WHAT IF YOUR LAWYER ISN'T REALLY A LAWYER?

In July 1998, The New York Times reported that a con man with no legal degree served as a lawyer for perhaps 100 defendants. This was said to be good news for convicted defendants and bad news for prosecutors. At first glance, this seems backward. Would you be happy to hear that your cardiac surgeon is a fraud?

The reason convicted defendants were happy is because this news entitled them to retrials. The Constitution guarantees accused criminals a defense conducted by a licensed attorney. Because in this instance their counsel was not really an attorney, convicted defendants could demand a new trial (with an authentic attorney, of course). Though the law is not clear on the subject, in all likelihood defendants needed not even show that their ersatz attorney was incompetent. (Initial reports suggest that, in fact, he was quite competent.) It is enough to show that he was not licensed. For example, defendants represented by disbarred attorneys have been awarded retrials without proving that their defense was inadequate.

What's so great about a retrial? It is true that in principle, a retrial can still result in a conviction. But if prosecution witnesses have died or forgotten things, then their testimony won't be used in the retrial. Even transcripts from the previous trial can't be used in the retrial, since they were admitted when the defendant had inadequate counsel.

IS A CANADIAN SAME-SEX MARRIAGE VALID IN THE UNITED STATES?

Gay and lesbian couples flocked to Ontario courthouses in 2003 after a Canadian appeals court struck down that province's ban on same-sex marriages. The United States acknowledges Canadian marriages as legally valid. If a gay or lesbian American couple gets hitched north of the border, will their union be recognized back home?

Probably not, at least until the newlyweds pursue the matter through the courts. The United States recognizes most foreign marriages because of comity, the legal version of the Golden Rule. The principle holds that lawful conduct in one jurisdiction should be respected in another, lest travelers worry about their marriages being invalidated as they cross borders. But comity is more a custom than an obligation, and neither the states nor the federal government are compelled to extend the courtesy to every couple wed abroad. They can decline if the marriage in question violates a jurisdiction's definition of an acceptable union—say, if the bride is below the age of consent or if the couple are close blood relations. Or, in the case of same-sex marriages, if a local law explicitly defines marriage as a union between a man and a woman. The latter stipulation is a key part of the Defense of Marriage Act (DOMA), signed by President Clinton in 1996. The law bars federal recognition of same-sex marriages, regardless of whether those unions are deemed legally valid in another country or even in an individual state. So same-sex couples wed in Canada have no shot, for example, at being able to file their federal taxes jointly. In addition, thirty-seven states have passed similarly worded legislation.

That leaves thirteen states where Canadian same-sex unions may eventually be recognized, although gay couples would likely need to take legal action to earn full privileges—for example, by suing for family health benefits. If one state does yield, however, it will create an entirely new set of legal questions. States are bound by the Constitution's full faith and credit clause to recognize the "public acts, records, and judicial proceedings" of one another. How the courts will weigh that clause against the state's DOMA is anyone's guess. Currently, several couples who've entered into civil unions in Vermont, the only state to permit such a marriagelike arrangement, are suing for recognition in their home states on full faith and credit grounds; none of the cases has yet been resolved.

Bonus Explainer: Canada is not the world's first nation with a province that permits same-sex marriages. The Netherlands legalized such unions in 2001, although the country doesn't make it easy for Americans to take advantage. One half of the couple must first establish residency, typically by living in Holland for at least four months.

DO DEAD AUTHORS HOLD ON TO THEIR COPYRIGHTS?

True at First Light, *the fourth posthumous publication of Ernest Hemingway's writings, was released on the hundredth anniversary of the author's birth. It came on the heels of* Juneteenth, *a posthumous novel assembled from notes and stories by Ralph Ellison. Both books sparked questions about the ethics of publishing an author's unfinished works after he has died. Is there any legal action a writer can take while living to keep his unpublished works out of the public eye forever?*

Copyright laws provide some defense, but they're hardly airtight. A copyright gives a living author control over his original work, published or not, including exclusive rights to reproductions, distribution, and displays of the work. Anyone who violates a creator's copyright can be sued by the copyright holder. In the United States, the copyright protection extends for seventy years following the creator's death, with the right of enforcement falling to the creator's estate or designated agent. So you could stipulate in your will that you don't want your works published, or you could leave the copyright to some person or organization with instructions not to publish them.

But those works would be protected for only seventy years before being released into the public domain (that is, before they can be reproduced freely by the public). Besides, there's little to prevent your executor from publishing the works anyway. In theory, a suit could be brought against a copyright holder who published against an author's wishes *if* the author's will explicitly stated that he didn't want that to happen—and assuming, of course, that someone among the living would file the suit. So if you really don't want your unpublished manuscripts to see the light of day, you need to destroy them before the bell tolls for you.

MEDICINE

HOW DOES **ALZHEIMER'S DISEASE KILL?**

HORSES HAVE A **WEST NILE VACCINE.** WHY DON'T WE?

WHAT ARE **EAR ROCKS?**

WHAT IS **CONSUMPTION?**

WHAT ARE THE **RULES** FOR EXPERIMENTING **ON HUMANS?**

HOW IS **RITALIN** LIKE COCAINE?

HORSES HAVE A WEST NILE VACCINE. WHY DON'T WE?

Tens of thousands of horses are being vaccinated against the West Nile virus. A human version of the vaccine likely won't be available for a decade, if ever. Why do horses have the pharmaceutical edge in the fight against West Nile?

Our animal friends are benefiting from the relative laxity of federal veterinary regulations. In August 2001, the U.S. Department of Agriculture (USDA) gave conditional approval to an equine vaccine manufactured by Fort Dodge Animal Health, a division of Wyeth. Though the product's safety had been thoroughly proved, its efficacy against West Nile had not. But the USDA judged the virus to be a crisis, since horses are particularly susceptible—about a third of infected horses will perish, compared with around 10 percent of humans who exhibit symptoms. The agency thus exercised its right to grant an emergency okay for the vaccine's sale. About 2 million shots have been sold nationwide since then, at upward of $30 a pop.

The Food and Drug Administration is not similarly lenient when it comes to human vaccines, even for high-profile maladies like West Nile. Regardless of public paranoia, a vaccine's efficacy must be demonstrated over three phases of human clinical trials before earning the FDA's seal of approval. Researchers from the National Institute of Allergy and Infectious Diseases reported in March that they'd successfully vaccinated mice against the virus; they'll have to repeat their results in monkeys before moving on to clinical trials with humans. A private company called Acambis is a bit further along with its West Nile vaccine. But even perfect results won't get Acambis's shot into your doctor's offices before 2006 or 2007.

There's no need to envy the horses quite yet, as the jury's still out on how helpful Fort Dodge's vaccine really is long-term. But some zookeepers aren't waiting around for additional data. Burned by West Nile deaths among their exotic birds in 2001, several zoos administered the equine vaccine to their avian populations. The

Houston Zoo, for example, has vaccinated its flamingos and Att-water's prairie chickens.

HOW DOES ALZHEIMER'S DISEASE KILL?

A New York Times obituary for elections analyst Richard Scammon listed his cause of death as Alzheimer's disease. How does this illness cause death?

Death by Alzheimer's disease, a progressive brain disorder char-acterized by loss of memory, is usually caused by secondary infec-tions that are common in incapacitated patients. There are about 4 million Americans with the disease, and the average length of time between diagnosis and death is eight years, although people can live with the illness twenty years or more. As the disease pro-gresses, patients lose the ability to coordinate basic motor skills such as swallowing, walking, or controlling bladder and bowel. Difficulty swallowing can cause food to be inhaled, which can result in pneumonia. Inability to walk can lead to bedsores. Incontinence can result in bladder infections. These infections become particularly difficult to deal with because Alzheimer's patients are unable to understand and participate in their own treatment. While reports say that former president Ronald Rea-gan, an Alzheimer's sufferer, is recovering well from his broken hip, such falls often lead to death because the patient does not have the capacity to follow directions or the motivation to try to walk again. Such incapacitation again sets the stage for deadly infections. Doctors say it is possible that an Alzheimer's patient could progress to the point that damage from the disease to the centers of the brain that control breathing could cause death, but patients rarely get that far without an infection setting in. Once a patient is extremely incapacitated, there is little medical motiva-tion to aggressively treat such infections.

In 2002, Alzheimer's disease was the eighth leading cause of death in the United States, with 49,044 deaths, and the fifth leading cause for people 85 and up. Experts say Alzheimer's deaths have been historically underreported because infections such as pneumonia were listed on death certificates instead of Alzheimer's.

WHAT ARE EAR ROCKS?

Jamal Mashburn, a forward for the Charlotte and New Orleans Hornets, missed important games in the 2002 NBA play-offs with positional vertigo. What is positional vertigo, and how do you treat it?

Positional vertigo feels like a wave of dizziness and nausea, as if the sufferer has just stepped off a high-speed merry-go-round. It's caused by loose calcium carbonate crystals—or ear rocks—floating about the inner ear. The ear rocks are dislodged from a sac in the inner ear by head injuries, viruses (as in Mashburn's case), or degeneration of the ear (as in most patients over 50). When the head is tilted, the rocks rub against nerve endings that affect balance.

Doctors sometimes prescribe sedatives like Valium to alleviate the symptoms. But a pharmacological approach was not appropriate in Mashburn's case; it would be tough to crash the boards while doped up on chill pills. Instead, doctors treated the star forward by performing a series of maneuvers designed to nudge the ear rocks back into place. The most popular of these exercises is the so-called Epley maneuver, which involves sequential side-to-side head movements (occasionally aided by a vibrator placed behind the ear). About 75 percent of patients are cured after a single 10-minute session, provided they spend the following two nights sleeping with their heads tilted at a 45-degree angle.

But Mashburn's ear rocks seemed particularly stubborn. He had to perform a more rigorous set of maneuvers, which usually involve three sets of head twists and full-body flops per day. The program has a 95 percent cure rate, but it takes at least two weeks to complete. In extremely rare cases, when exercise fails, the calcium crystals must be immobilized through a surgical procedure, which can lead to partial deafness.

WHAT ARE THE RULES FOR EXPERIMENTING ON HUMANS?

Federal regulators temporarily shut down Johns Hopkins University's human medical research program in July 2001 following the death of a healthy woman in an asthma study. What regulations govern federally funded medical research involving human subjects, and what did Johns Hopkins do wrong?

Sixteen federal departments and agencies, ranging from the National Science Foundation and the Department of Health and Human Services to the Department of Defense and the Central Intelligence Agency, adopted a common federal policy in 1991 for the protection of human research subjects. (The Food and Drug Administration has its own policy.) A human subject is defined as any "living individual about whom an investigator (whether professional or student) conducting research obtains (1) data through intervention or interaction with the individual, or (2) identifiable private information." Even mundane research conducted with paper-and-pencil questionnaires qualifies as human experimentation. (Though some research involving surveys or interviews is exempt from federal regulations.) The regulations authorize institutional review boards (IRBs), local review panels at research institutions, with overseeing human research. IRBs can approve, modify, or reject all research within their jurisdiction. Some institutions, including Johns Hopkins, have more than one IRB. Many IRBs also review research exempt from federal regulations.

IRBs draw their members from many different professions in addition to the sciences. One member's primary concern must be scientific, and one member's primary concern must be nonscientific, to ensure that the IRB is competent to review both science and ethics. The members must be free of any conflicts of interest regarding the research when they vote. Strict documentation is also required, including the recording of IRB minutes. IRB records must be retained for at least three years. As one guide to the requirements puts it, "If it isn't documented, it didn't happen."

Institutions that conduct human research must provide a written assurance that they will meet federal standards. The assurance must also contain a statement of principles. In the United States, most assurances cite the Belmont Report, a 1978 study by the National Commission for the Protection of Human Subjects of Biomedical and Behavioral Research. The report sets forth three basic ethical principles governing medical research on human subjects: respect for persons, beneficence, and justice. Respect for persons requires informed consent, beneficence requires the minimization of risks and a risk-benefit analysis, and justice requires the fair and equitable selection of subjects, in order to prevent the burden of research from falling on the poor or the disadvantaged, as it did in the Tuskegee syphilis study. The Belmont Report also states that brutal or inhumane treatment is never morally justified, that research must be conducted by qualified investigators using appropriate designs, and that subjects must be free to withdraw at any time.

Children who cannot consent legally must still provide assent to participate, and their parents or guardians must also grant permission. The need for informed consent is why some researchers prefer the term *participants* to *subjects.* Because of informed consent requirements, there are specific regulations for research involving prisoners, children, and fetuses and pregnant women.

WHAT IS CONSUMPTION?

In the film Moulin Rouge, *set at the turn of the nineteenth century, Nicole Kidman plays a courtesan who looks great while suffering from a cough caused by consumption. Just what is consumption, how deadly is it, and is it still around?*

The word *consumption* first appeared in the fourteenth century to describe any potentially fatal wasting disease—that is, any condition that consumed the body. But over time it came to apply more specifically to tuberculosis. Although the word *tuberculosis* first appeared in 1860, it wasn't until 1882 that German physician Robert Koch identified the rod-shaped bacterium that caused the illness. While tuberculosis can affect many parts of the body, such as the bones or digestive tract, its greatest affinity is for the lungs. When actively infected people cough or sneeze, they spread droplets that can be inhaled by others. It usually takes prolonged contact to contract an infection, and even then the immune systems of healthy people can effectively contain the exposure. But in people with an active late-stage case of TB, the lung tissue gets eaten away by rapidly expanding colonies of bacteria. Victims may experience weight loss, fever, night sweats, and coughing up of blood-filled sputum. Despite the movies, it is not a pretty way to die.

Tuberculosis was a great killer at the time *Moulin Rouge* is set, during a period when many poor people crowded together in rapidly expanding cities. Occurrence began to decrease with better sanitation, housing, and nutrition, and an understanding of how to control the spread of the disease. Then, in the 1940s, antibiotic treatment brought a cure and rapid decline of TB incidence. But it remains deadly, particularly in many parts of the developing world. The 1980s also brought a resurgence in the West with the occurrence of AIDS, which damages the body's ability to fight TB, and with the advent of antibiotic-resistant strains of the disease.

TB has a long artistic pedigree. Greta Garbo was a consumptive courtesan who expired exquisitely in the movie *Camille* in 1936. That film was based on Dumas's *La Dame aux Camélias,* which also inspired the Verdi opera *La Traviata.* Puccini's *La Bohème* also features a heroine dying of consumption. Thomas Mann's novel *The Magic Mountain* is set in a tuberculosis sanitarium, and Chekhov, in his first play, *Ivanov,* features a wife dying of the disease. TB also ended many artistic lives, including those of Chekhov, Chopin, Kafka, Keats, and Orwell.

HOW IS RITALIN LIKE COCAINE?

A report in the January 2003 issue of Pediatrics *concluded that children treated with Ritalin are not more likely to abuse drugs as adults. A* New York Times *rundown of the report noted that Ritalin is "chemically similar to cocaine." Just how similar?*

Both cocaine and methylphenidate, the generic name for Ritalin, are stimulants that target the dopamine system, which helps control the brain's functioning during pleasurable experiences. The two drugs block the ability of neurons to reabsorb dopamine, thus flooding the brain with a surplus of the joy-inducing neurotransmitter. According to animal studies, Ritalin and cocaine act so much alike that they even compete for the same binding sites on neurons.

Why, then, aren't the 4 million to 6 million kids who take Ritalin daily acting more like the Studio 54 crowd, circa 1977? One important difference is that Ritalin, administered as directed, acts much more slowly than cocaine. Nora Volkow, a senior scientist at Brookhaven National Laboratory who has done extensive research on methylphenidate, found in a 2001 study that Ritalin takes upward of an hour to raise dopamine levels; cocaine, mere seconds. The exact reason why the uptake speed matters is unknown, but it seems to account for the different effects.

Note, however, that not all Ritalin users swallow their pills. Recreational users frequently crush their supply into fine powder for nasal delivery or, in extreme cases, melt it into an injectable solution. These administration methods increase the speed of uptake, and users report that the high is not too terribly different from a cocaine buzz.

The exact nature of the experience depends on each person's unique brain chemistry; those who naturally lack an adequate amount of dopamine, such as people diagnosed with attention-deficit/hyperactivity disorder, may feel less giddy than a nonsufferer. And about half of Ritalin users who don't have ADHD won't enjoy the kick, which can be comparable to ingesting one (or six) too many espressos.

STRANGE CAREERS

WHAT'S THE MOST **POWERFUL** POLITICAL JOB **IN CHINA?**

HOW DO YOU **BECOME** A WEAPONS INSPECTOR?

WHO DO YOU CALL **WHEN YOU FIND A TICKING NUKE?**

WHY DOES THE **CIA** HAVE CONTRACT EMPLOYEES?

DO **TV TALK-SHOW** GUESTS GET PAID?

WHY DO **PRIZED POOCHES** HAVE WEIRD NAMES?

HOW DO YOU BECOME A WEAPONS INSPECTOR?

The UN Security Council approved a resolution in 2002 calling for renewed weapons inspections in Iraq. How do you become a UN weapons inspector?

An extensive background in chemical engineering, missile design, or bacteriology is a good start. Inspectors are expected to recognize the telltale signs of covert weapons production, such as machine tools that have multiple uses or trace elements of lethal chemicals. Missile inspectors typically have worked for defense contractors, and thus can inspect metallurgical debris to determine whether it's left over from a hastily disassembled factory. Nuclear arms specialists may have spent time in uranium enrichment plants, which gives them a leg up on identifying the widgets necessary to build an A-bomb. Molecular pharmacologists and microbiologists are brought on board to figure out whether a seemingly innocuous pill mill has the capacity to churn out the bubonic plague. Advanced degrees aren't always required, but they don't hurt.

In Iraq, there were a few slots available for database experts, who matched up old sales records with current Iraqi inventories. Translators fluent in Arabic were welcome, too. And there was room for one or two intelligence experts, whose job it was to sift through the conflicting tales told by Iraqi scientists and parse out the truth.

Potential inspectors are encouraged to send their résumés to the UN Monitoring, Verification, and Inspection Commission, which organizes the inspections. Headquartered in New York City, UNMOVIC conducts periodic training sessions for new inspectors. In late 2002, the commission already had 220 experts from forty-four nations on call. The largest contingent came from France.

Inspection work is largely tedious, but being a UNMOVIC

employee carries some nice perks. The pay is quite decent (the average UN worker's salary is more than $100,000); there's tons of travel and—per the UN custom—lots of holidays. Many UNMOVIC applicants are government employees in their homelands, where their posts aren't nearly as rewarding. Or, one suspects, as potentially dangerous.

WHAT'S THE MOST POWERFUL POLITICAL JOB IN CHINA?

Hu Jintao was named general secretary of China's Communist Party in November 2002, replacing the long-serving Jiang Zemin. Hu later added the title of president when Jiang officially relinquished that post, too. Jiang, however, continues to helm the nation's central military commission. What do all these titles mean?

The general secretary's job is by far the most significant of the troika, since the Communist Party is ultimately responsible for all China's political, economic, and legal institutions. Hu is also the senior member of the nine-member (formerly seven-member) politburo standing committee, an oligarchic group charged with setting all national policies. The general secretary cannot act unilaterally, but he has considerable latitude to shape the committee's agenda and steer the party's political philosophy—although Hu initially vowed not to deviate from the path outlined by his predecessor.

The presidency is primarily a ceremonial post, elected by the 2,979 members of the National People's Congress (albeit with a very firm nudge from the Communist leadership). However, it is key for a party secretary to cement his power by adding president to his collection of titles. The chairmanship of the military commission is the third jewel of China's political crown, and a post from which aging figures like to continue their string-pulling ways. As was the case with his predecessor, Deng Xiaoping, the elderly Jiang's insistence on retaining control of the world's largest army signals that he won't be going so gently into that good night.

Though he is no longer an official member of the politburo standing committee, Jiang will leverage his military command to influence the party's direction.

Though titles are important to keeping score in Chinese politics, they rarely tell the whole story. Hua Guofeng, Mao Ze-dong's handpicked successor, garnered all three main titles subsequent to his mentor's death. But Deng, a master of backroom power grabs, had little trouble squeezing out the weaker Hua.

Bonus Explainer: Another key job in the Chinese power game is premier, which is far less glamorous than it sounds. Unlike Western parliamentary leaders, who often double as heads of state, a Chinese premier—invariably a member of the politburo standing committee—is responsible for ensuring the smooth functioning of the bureaucracy. There's relatively little political glory in ensuring that local officials in Lanzhou are performing up to snuff.

WHO DO YOU CALL WHEN YOU FIND A TICKING NUKE?

Who will protect us if a ticking nuke turns up in downtown Washington or New York City?

The Nuclear Emergency Search Team, or NEST. President Gerald Ford created this special response team following a 1974 nuclear extortion hoax in Boston. NEST consists of roughly 1,000 Energy Department physicists, engineers, and computer programmers who have volunteered for training. NEST members, who are on 24-7 call, are scattered around the country. In the event of an emergency, NEST can mobilize a team within four hours. (NESTers are unarmed; the FBI or commandos carry the iron.)

It's next to impossible to find a bomb without some clue about where to look. But portable gamma-ray and neutron detectors can sniff out some nukes from vans or helicopters. After narrowing down the location of a bomb, NEST members seek the device as surreptitiously as possible using portable radiation detectors hidden inside briefcases, backpacks, or as some reports claim, beer coolers. (The terrorists could shield their weapon's radiation with lead, but that would dramatically increase the device's weight.) Background radiation can also complicate a search, which is why Energy Department scientists map natural radiation hot spots created by things such as hospital equipment.

To disable the weapon, NEST must determine whether it is dealing with a nuclear bomb or a dirty bomb, in which radioactive materials have been attached to conventional explosives. Dirty bombs are less destructive than nuclear bombs but are still extremely deadly. They are likely to be easier to disarm, however, because they are based on cruder technology. NEST can contain the blast from a dirty bomb by erecting huge nylon tents around it and adding chemical foam to absorb radioactive material if the device explodes. The first step in deactivating a nuclear bomb is to divine its structure with X-rays and compare it against potential bomb designs. The dismantlers start by checking for booby traps. They're said to carry 30 mm cannons to shoot a bomb to bits, liquid nitrogen to freeze a bomb's electronics, and high-pressure water jets that can carve a weapon without creating dangerous sparks.

NEST refuses to discuss reports of its deployments, but according to published reports, the team has been alerted about 110 times up to 1998; 30 of those threats were deemed credible. In one, a former nuclear plant employee stole deadly uranium oxide and threatened to disperse it unless he was paid $100,000. (He was caught and jailed.) The *San Jose Mercury News* has cited several other NEST responses, including a 1987 bomb threat in Indianapolis and one in El Paso, Texas, in 1990.

Although NEST is staffed by some of the nation's best and brightest, it is only as good as the intelligence that leads it to bombs. In 1997, the Energy Department told Congress that when NEST was created, the assumption was that nuclear extortionists would allow time for negotiations, giving NEST time to hunt. "The idea that a terrorist would gain possession of a nuclear device and detonate it without warning was not deemed credible," the agency said. It is now.

WHY DOES THE CIA HAVE CONTRACT EMPLOYEES?

A missionary-bearing airplane shot down over Peru in April 2001 was first identified as suspicious by a crew of Central Intelligence Agency contract employees flying on an antidrug surveillance mission. Why does the CIA have contract employees, and what do they do?

Hiring contract employees makes bureaucratic sense. It allows the CIA to expand its workforce cheaply, since contract employees don't get the health insurance or retirement benefits regular employees are entitled to. It also allows the agency the flexibility of hiring specialists in, say, aerial surveillance in the Amazon jungle without having to retain them after the mission ends. The CIA does not release a head count of its full-time or contract employees, but hiring contractors is a long-standing, widespread practice. Such temporary workers are often found in the field, particularly in programs to monitor drug trafficking abroad. But a contractor could be hired for more mundane work, such as providing foreign language translation at headquarters.

Contractors can be detailed to work for the CIA from other organizations—for instance, employees of a company that has a contract with the agency to do surveillance work. Contractors are supposed to go through security processing similar to that required of regular CIA employees. And like CIA employees, they are supposed to know only what they need to know about what they are working on. While the CIA has acknowledged the role of its contractors in the Peruvian missionary disaster, it usually does not comment on whether an individual—whether a contractor or a regular employee—is affiliated with the agency. Normally contractors are not supposed to reveal their connection, either. If someone is a CIA contract employee looking for drug traffickers in South America, it's not considered a good idea to announce that fact—particularly if the agency isn't providing health insurance.

DO TV TALK-SHOW GUESTS GET PAID?

Gore Vidal famously said, "Never turn down a chance to have sex or go on television." Do people who go on TV talk shows get paid?

The answer is, it depends—primarily on whether the particular TV show is classified as entertainment or news. When millionaire actor Matt Damon goes on the *Tonight Show with Jay Leno* to promote his latest movie, he gets paid. When ubiquitous law professor Jonathan Turley appears on *Meet the Press*, it is for the glory alone. (Of course TV glory can lead to lucrative speeches and book contracts, so there is money in the act indirectly.)

Most late-night talk shows are considered entertainment. Everyone who appears on *Leno* or *Letterman* is paid at least the American Federation of Television and Radio Actors (AFTRA) minimum, which is $726 per episode.

On the other hand, anything produced by a network news department or a cable news network is thought of as news and doesn't pay. Conveniently, the news media regard paying interview guests as equivalent to paying sources, and therefore unethical. This category includes newsmagazines (*20/20, 60 Minutes*), evening newscasts (*CBS Evening News*, PBS's *NewsHour with Jim Lehrer*), Sunday talk shows (*Meet the Press, This Week*), daily scratch-and-bite shows (*Crossfire, Nightline*), and morning talk shows (*Good Morning America, Today*). So when Bob Dole appears with Jay Leno, he is paid; but if he shows up on *Meet the Press,* he isn't. And when a professional homemaker appears on *Today* to bake gingerbread, she's news and isn't paid.

A news show host (for example, Dan Rather or Tom Brokaw) is salaried, of course. So is anyone identified as a regular commentator, like ABC's George Will, who appears on *This Week*. Regular commentators receive yearly salaries and often appear on a variety of a network's shows. Panelists on weekly discussion shows like *McLaughlin Group* are also paid. Regulars are paid varying amounts; occasional panelists, on *McLaughlin* at least, get a few hundred dollars per episode.

Daytime talk shows like *Jerry Springer* follow the news model—that is, they don't pay. But they do cover expenses like airplane tickets, meals, and hotels. Oprah, among others, makes an exception for performers—meaning established TV or movie stars—who are given the AFTRA minimum.

In other countries, such as Britain, all broadcast guests get paid something—down to the five-minute radio interview subject. British journalists are often shocked to discover that American TV shows expect them to perform for free. Nevertheless, they rarely decline to appear. American journalists are often shocked to be offered money by foreign news services, such as the BBC and Canadian TV. Nevertheless, they rarely decline the check.

WHY DO PRIZED POOCHES HAVE WEIRD NAMES?

The coveted Best in Show title at 2003's Westminster Kennel Club Dog Show was snagged by a Kerry blue terrier named Ch. Torums Scarf Michael. Other top entrants included Ch. Set'R Ridge Wyndswept In Gold; Ch. Yakee Leaving Me BreathlessAtFranshaw; and Ch. Luxor's Playmate Of The Year. What does the doggy set have against classic names like Fido and Spike?

Nothing, really. In fact, Ch. Torums Scarf Michael is most commonly referred to by his call name, Mick; address him by the longer appellation, and there's no guarantee he'll come running. The multisyllabic tongue twisters are the formal names submitted to the American Kennel Club (AKC), with which every Westminster competitor must be registered. Only purebred dogs merit AKC papers and are thus allowed to register a name no longer than twenty-five letters (including apostrophes and spaces). So an extended, slightly aristocratic-sounding name is a badge of honor among dog aficionados—a symbol that their canine is a cut above the common mutt. The names are also often intensely personal, referring to a dog's hygienic habits, a deceased loved one, or a favorite fictional character.

Other naming guidelines include a ban on Arabic numerals, as well as the words *stud, sire, male,* and *female.* The prefix Ch. is an abbreviation for champion, denoting that the dog in question has won at least two major show titles overseen by different judges; every entrant at Westminster, the Olympics of the dog circuit, must be a champion. Some dogs also bear suffixes referring to their acumen in field trials, competitions in which dogs are judged on their ability to perform tasks rather than on pure beauty. The suffix appended to Ch. Magic Sir-ly You Jest JH, a Brittany, indicates that he's a junior hunter. Oftentimes, the first word of a dog's name makes reference to the kennel where he or she was bred. The first name of 2003's champ, Torum, is a celebrated British kennel. Also, words are sometimes intentionally misspelled to wiggle them into the 25-letter limitation, or to avoid repetition with another dog. (Thus an abundance of *y*'s in lieu of *i*'s.) And cheeky professional breeders sometimes go the theme route, naming an entire litter after varieties of candy or cheesy pop tunes.

The dogs' informal call names, strangely enough, often have nothing to do with the registered name. There's a connection between Ch. Torum's Scarf Michael and his call name, Mick. But Ch. Braeburn's Close Encounter's call name is Shannon, and only the owners know why.

THE MIDEAST

WHAT IS
**THE ARAB
LEAGUE?**

WHY IS THE
**FERTILE
CRESCENT**
SO INFERTILE?

WHAT DOES A
THUMBS-UP
MEAN IN IRAQ?

DID
SADDAM
IMPOSE A MUSTACHE
MANDATE?

WHY ARE SO MANY
BAGHDAD
LANDMARKS
NAMED RASHID?

WHY IS THE
MUSLIM HAJJ
SO DANGEROUS?

WHAT IS THE ARAB LEAGUE?

In March 2002, delegates to the Arab League summit in Beirut, Lebanon, discussed Saudi Crown Prince Abdullah's Middle East peace initiative. What is the Arab League?

The League of Arab States, as it is formally known, was founded in 1945 and considers itself the world's oldest regional organization. According to its website, its aims are "maximum integration among the Arab countries through coordination of their activities in the political sphere as well as in the fields of economics, social services, education, communications, development, technology and industrialization." The league has twenty-two members: Algeria, Bahrain, Comoros, Djibouti, Egypt, Iraq, Jordan, Kuwait, Lebanon, Libya, Mauritania, Morocco, Oman, Palestine, Qatar, Saudi Arabia, Somalia, Sudan, Syria, Tunisia, the United Arab Emirates, and Yemen. Egypt's membership was suspended in 1979 after it signed a peace treaty with Israel, but it was readmitted in 1989 and now dominates the organization, along with Saudi Arabia.

It has been almost impossible for members to agree on anything other than opposition to the state of Israel. The Palestine Liberation Organization was founded at the league's 1964 summit, and in the 1967 meeting, just three months after the Six Day War, the league rejected an Israeli peace proposal that would have returned the Sinai to Egypt and the Golan Heights to Syria. In doing so, it established the "three nos" policy: no to recognition of Israel, no to negotiations with Israel, and no to peace with Israel. According to the *Jerusalem Post,* "the Khartoum conference led to another generation of bloodshed in the Middle East." In the Cold War years, the league was divided between Soviet-affiliated states and Western allies, and there are also long-standing splits between the league's monarchies and its republics. During the

1990s, there were no Arab League summits because of lingering resentments between Kuwait and Iraq.

The Arab League has been somewhat revitalized by the appointment of Egyptian diplomat Amr Moussa as secretary-general in May 2001. Moussa pledged to focus on economic cooperation with the aim of making the league more like the European Union or Mercosur; however, since only about 8 percent of the Arab states' trade is with other Arab nations, there seems little hope for a common market.

WHY IS THE FERTILE CRESCENT SO INFERTILE?

The plains between the Tigris and Euphrates rivers supposedly mark the start of the Fertile Crescent, a strip of agriculturally rich land that runs through the Middle East. Yet during the war in Iraq, TV cameras showed little but sandstorms, bone-dry landscapes, and Iraqis crying out plaintively for water. Why isn't the Fertile Crescent more fertile? Why would the earliest societies have sprung up in such an arid, forbidding place?

The land between the Tigris and the Euphrates, south of Baghdad, can be categorized as silt desert: It is dry, yet very rich from millions of years of river deposits. When the Sumerian civilization, the first in the region, arose in 3,500 B.C., there was a bit more rainfall but not much. So the Sumerians, like every civilization in the area since, had to rely on extensive irrigation systems. In fact, some scholars think that the ingenuity, hard work, and administrative responsibility required to construct a system of canals helped train the Sumerians in state-building.

Because the land is so fragile, civilizations have periodically lost control of it. The Sumerians (who lived near modern Basra and Nasiriyah) gave way to the Babylonians, who lived farther north. They and their successors—the Hellenistic Seleucid rulers, then Iranian Parthians—continued to build huge canal systems. Early Arab rulers kept them going until the 1200s, when the system, which had seen many partial failures, finally collapsed. From the fifteenth to the twentieth century, the agricultural belt from Baghdad to Basra returned to desert.

(In another challenge to farmers, the land to the south of Baghdad also tends to be flat, with a hard subsurface three or four feet beneath the topsoil. During irrigation, water pools, and the subsequent evaporation leaves behind salt. This salinization can also ruin cropland. The solution is to leave the land fallow periodically.)

Modern Iraq has restored agriculture in its southeast (north of Nasiriyah, for instance), but that area has never fully recovered. Farming thrives around Baghdad, where growers cultivate everything from wheat to dates to tomatoes to tea. Kurdistan, to the north, is quite lush, too.

The rest of the Fertile Crescent—a term coined by University of Chicago anthropologist James H. Breasted in the early 1900s—receives much more rain than the portion the Americans marched through. The verdant ribbon of land continues into Syria, then down the Jordan River to the Mediterranean. Some scholars even include the rich but very narrow Nile Valley as part of the crescent, too.

WHAT DOES A THUMBS-UP MEAN IN IRAQ?

During the second Gulf War, Iraqis gave passing Americans the thumbs-up sign, which the troops interpreted as a symbol of support. But many veteran travelers insisted that the gesture is a crass Middle Eastern insult. How should coalition forces have taken those skyward thumbs?

Depends on how media savvy those Iraqi bystanders were. It's true that thumbs-up traditionally translates as the foulest of Iraqi insults—the most straightforward interpretation is "Up yours, pal!" The sign has a similarly pejorative meaning in parts of West

Africa, Russia, Australia, Iran, Greece, and Sardinia, according to Roger E. Axtell's book *Gestures: The Do's and Taboos of Body Language Around the World*. So it's possible that the ostensibly cheering Iraqis were, in fact, silently voicing their displeasure.

But it's also possible that they understood the Western meaning of upturned thumbs, an explanation that the Army's Defense Language Institute subscribes to. According to a recent DLI manual on international gestures, after the first Gulf War, "Middle Easterners of the Arabian Peninsula adopted this hand movement, along with the OK sign, as a symbol of cooperation toward freedom." Iraqi civilians may have noted this shifting meaning, perhaps via TV reports.

How the thumbs-up became an upbeat gesture in the first place is something of a mystery. Legend has it that the signal dates back to Roman gladiatorial contests. A beaten combatant could supposedly be saved from a death blow if the emperor gave the thumbs-up; a thumbs-down was tantamount to a death sentence. Though a favorite of Hollywood "swords and sandals" epics, this explanation has been completely debunked in recent years. In 1997, University of Kansas classics professor Anthony Philip Corbeill concluded that the thumbs-up actually meant "Kill him," basing his assertion on a study of hundreds of ancient artworks. Instead, he wrote, a closed fist with a thumb wrapped around it was the indication for a gladiator's life to be spared.

No one's quite sure about where the positive American connotation comes from, though a good guess ascribes it to an English symbol of agreement. Desmond Morris's *Gestures: Their Origins and Distribution* traces the practice back to a medieval custom used to seal business transactions. The two involved parties would lick their thumbs, hold them erect, then smush them together. Over time, the mere sight of an upraised thumb came to symbolize harmony and kind feelings.

The gesture's popularization in America is generally attributed to the practices of World War II pilots, who used the thumbs-up to communicate with ground crews prior to takeoff. American GIs are reputed to have picked up on the thumb and spread it throughout Europe as they marched toward Berlin.

DID SADDAM IMPOSE A MUSTACHE MANDATE?

Expertly manicured mustaches seem to be ubiquitous among Iraqi men, particularly those who served in Saddam Hussein's inner circle. Was the hirsuteness a Saddam-mandated requirement or merely part of Iraqi tradition?

Mostly the latter. Iraqi men have taken tremendous pride in their mustaches since at least the sixteenth century, when the whisker-loving Ottomans ruled the region. The bushier the better is the general rule of thumb, as mustache thickness is believed to be directly proportional to masculinity. As *Newsday* correspondent Matthew McAllester noted, an impressive man is often complimented with the adage "an eagle could land on his mustache."

Mustaches also serve as metaphors for personal honor. Iraqi men will swear on them, much as many Americans will swear on a Bible, and to tug a rival's mustache is tantamount to the slap of a glove on an opponent's face. In March 2002, at an Islamic summit in Doha, Qatar, an Iraqi official insulted a Kuwaiti heckler by shouting, "Curse be upon your mustache, you traitor!"

Saddam Hussein's preference for a Stalinesque mustache only increased the look's popularity, of course. During the Iran-Iraq War, young conscripts were urged to grow Saddam-like facial hair—partly in homage to their president and partly to differentiate themselves from the Iranian troops, who favored ayatollah-inspired beards. Given Saddam's suspicion of nonconformists, not to mention his wild megalomania, soldiers were well advised to mimic the dictator's grooming habits—which reportedly included frequent dye jobs to ward off unflattering gray.

WHY ARE SO MANY BAGHDAD LANDMARKS NAMED RASHID?

Saddam Hussein was quite fond of naming Baghdad landmarks after himself—in addition to battle-torn Saddam International Airport, there was Saddam Mosque, Saddam Central Hospital, and International Saddam Tower (topped with a revolving restaurant). But many of the city's most famous sites also bear the name Rashid— the Al-Rashid Hotel, Al-Rashid Street, and the Al-Rashid army base, to name a few. Who is Rashid, and why did Saddam spare these landmarks his eponymous touch?

Even an egoist of Saddam's stature knew that Rashid is a hallowed name among Iraqis, since it's shared by two of the nation's greatest icons. Fans of *The Book of the Thousand Nights and a Night* (also known as *Arabian Nights*) will recognize the name Harun al-Rashid, the fifth ruler of the Abbasid caliphate. Al-Rashid, whose reign lasted from A.D. 786 to 809, is renowned as the caliph who presided over Baghdad's golden age. A generous patron of the arts and sciences, he was immortalized in the fairy tales of Scheherazade, the storytelling narrator of *Arabian Nights*. When Saddam first ascended to the presidency in 1979, much of his early propaganda focused on drawing comparisons between himself and al-Rashid, as a way of convincing Iraqis that he'd lead them into a new era of greatness.

Then there's Rashid Ali al-Gailani, often hailed as the father of Iraqi nationalism. Throughout the 1930s, Iraq was essentially a client state of Great Britain, bound to the colonial power by a "cooperation pact." Though fervently anti-British, Rashid Ali (as he's popularly known) was named prime minister of Iraq in 1940; the following April, with German military assistance, he led a military coup against the Iraqi monarchy. His reign as a pan-Arab president lasted mere weeks, as the British swiftly moved to crush the revolt and secure their access to Iraq's oil. Rashid Ali fled, first to Iran, then to Nazi Germany and Saudi Arabia. He returned to his native land only after the 1958 revolution, which established the first Iraqi republic. Despite the brevity of his time in power, Rashid Ali remained a hero to Saddam's Baath Party.

WHY IS THE MUSLIM HAJJ SO DANGEROUS?

More than a dozen Muslim pilgrims were trampled to death in February 2003, while performing the annual hajj in Saudi Arabia. Such tragedies seem to occur with depressing frequency—since 1997, at least 570 worshippers have been accidentally killed during the annual trek to Mecca. Why is the hajj so dangerous?

Simply put, the ancient facilities have not expanded in proportion to the number of pilgrims. The most hazardous part of the hajj is the stoning of the pillars at Mina, which is where the most recent catastrophe took place. The ceremony, in which Muslims symbolically rebuke the devil by throwing twenty-one pebbles at three pillars, has changed little over the past fourteen centuries. What has changed is the number of participants—at least 2 million people a year now partake, according to unofficial estimates. That's thought to be a fourfold increase over the number of pilgrims who made the trip in 1970. The pillars, of course, have remained the same size, making access more difficult. Worshippers approach the pillars via the Jamarat Bridge, which can supposedly accommodate 100,000 pedestrians per hour. Yet the load often far exceeds this figure since, according to the rules of the hajj, the stoning ritual should be completed in a single day before sundown. It doesn't take much to initiate a deadly stampede under such overcrowded conditions. In 1998, for example, a panic ensued after a few pilgrims fell off the bridge; the ensuing melee killed 180. The February incident reportedly began when a group of worshippers failed to exit the area surrounding the pillars (the Al-Aqaba Jamarah) in a timely fashion, creating a crush when new pilgrims entered.

The stoning ritual is the most obviously dangerous part of the five-day event, but tragedies have occurred elsewhere in recent years, too. In 1997, 340 were killed and over 1,500 injured when a fire swept through a tent city pitched near Mina; tents are now required to be fireproof as a result. And in 1990, at least 1,400 were killed during a stampede in the 500-meter tunnel that connects Mecca to Mount Arafat, where Muhammad is believed to have delivered his last sermon. That disaster is often blamed on the panic caused by a faulty ventilation system.

Sensitive to these hazards, the Saudi Arabian government has tried its best to limit the hajj's dangers. The event is overseen by the Ministry of the Interior, which has recently instituted such reforms as monitoring crowd patterns from helicopters and equipping the Jamarat Bridge with surveillance cameras. At the heart of the Al-Aqaba Jamarah, the ministry's efforts include setting up medical units and blaring prerecorded messages over the loudspeakers, requesting that pilgrims depart in an orderly fashion. But even 20,000 security officers are not enough to ensure absolute safety, as evidenced by February's sad events. If there is a silver lining to be found, it might be that Muslim tradition holds that pilgrims killed during the hajj are guaranteed entry into paradise.

WHAT'S THE DIFFERENCE?

TOP SECRET.
CONFIDENTIAL.

PAPAL BULLS.
PAPAL ENCYCLICALS.

CEO.
CHAIRMAN.

PARDONS.
COMMUTATIONS.

GENOCIDE.

CRIMES AGAINST HUMANITY.

AGENT.
MANAGER.

TOP SECRET. CONFIDENTIAL.

News reports about the lost and found Los Alamos hard drives in 2000 variously described their contents as sensitive, secret, and confidential. Are these terms interchangeable? What is their significance?

The executive agencies sort classified information into three categories of escalating sensitivity: confidential, secret, and top secret. Confidential applies to information whose release could damage national security, whereas secret carries with it the potential for serious damage and top secret for grave damage. In practice, the definitions are flexible and each agency has adapted the terminology for its own use. About 25 percent of all newly classified documents fall into the confidential category. More than two-thirds are labeled secret, and the remainder—roughly 10 percent—are graded top secret.

While any information can be classified—documents, cable traffic, and information from other sources—the government mostly applies it to documents. In 1998, the federal government classified more than 7 million documents, with the CIA classifying 40 percent of them, the Defense Department 29 percent, the National Reconnaissance Office 27 percent, and the Justice Department 2 percent. (The State Department accounted for 1 percent of all classified documents, but that number does not include the hundreds of thousands of diplomatic cables sent each year.) The total number of classified documents is in the billions. In 1995, President Clinton signed an executive order requiring all new classified information to include a declassification date at its birth. All classified material older than twenty-five years had to be reviewed and, unless it met a narrow exemption, be declassified.

PAPAL BULLS. PAPAL ENCYCLICALS.

To clarify Pope John Paul II's position on stem-cell research, the Vatican quoted from his 1995 encyclical, Evangelium Vitae. *What's an encyclical, and how does it differ from a papal bull?*

The Catholic Church articulates and develops its teachings primarily through encyclicals. Traditionally, an encyclical is a letter from the pope to the church's bishops, but during the past forty years the pope has also addressed them to the faithful and to "all people of good will." Pope John Paul II has issued more than a dozen encyclicals, including 1998's *Fides et Ratio* ("Faith and Reason"). Notable encyclicals include Paul VI's 1968 *Humanae Vitae* ("On Human Life"), which affirmed the church's stance against contraception, and John Paul II's 1995 *Evangelium Vitae* ("The Gospel of Life"), which condemned the "culture of death" the pope saw manifested in abortion, euthanasia, and capital punishment. The first encyclical was circulated by Benedict XIV in 1740.

Prior to the eighteenth century, the church expressed its teachings through apostolic bulls, more legalistic and solemn documents than encyclicals. (Bull refers to the Latin *bulla*, or seal, which is affixed to the document.) The condemnation of Martin Luther, for example, came in a papal bull. Today, the Vatican issues bulls mostly to confer the titles of bishops and cardinals or to proclaim the canonization of a saint.

Encyclicals are authoritative, not to be criticized or rejected lightly by members of the church, but they are not infallible. Only three doctrines developed in the past two hundred years are considered infallible, and all were issued as bulls: the Immaculate Conception (that Mary was born without original sin), the Assumption (that Mary was taken up body and soul into heaven), and the definition of papal infallibility issued by the First Vatican Council.

CEO. CHAIRMAN.

In January 2000, Microsoft founder Bill Gates announced that he was handing over the job of CEO to the company's president, Steve Ballmer. Gates said that he would remain Microsoft's chairman. What's the difference between these two jobs? And which one is more powerful?

The CEO is a company's top decision-maker, and all other executives answer to him or her. The CEO typically delegates many of the tactical responsibilities to other managers, focusing instead on strategic issues, such as which markets to enter, how to take on the competition, and which companies to form partnerships with. This is in contrast to the chief operating officer or president, who oversees day-to-day operations and logistics. The CEO is ultimately accountable to the board of directors for the company's performance.

The chairman of a company is the head of its board of directors. The board is elected by shareholders and is responsible for protecting investors' interests, such as the company's profitability and stability. It usually meets several times a year to set long-term goals, review financial results, evaluate the performance of high-level managers, and vote on important strategic moves proposed by the CEO. Directors appoint and can fire upper-level managers such as the CEO and the president. The chairman typically wields substantial power in setting the board's agenda and determining the outcome of votes. But he or she does not necessarily play an active role in everyday management.

The balance of power between the CEO and the chairman varies widely from company to company. Because the CEO cannot make major moves without the board's assent, and his or her job security depends on their satisfaction, the chairman of the board is technically his or her superior. And an active chairman may use this power to effectively become the co-head—and ultimate boss—of the corporation. But most chairmen are not so involved, which leaves the CEO with considerable flexibility in running the company. The CEO can also affect the composition of the board of directors through his or her selection of senior executives, many of whom are guaranteed board seats by company bylaws. Sometimes—as was the case with Gates until 2000—the chairman and the CEO are the same person.

PARDONS. COMMUTATIONS.

President Clinton granted a spate of pardons and commutations at the end of his second term. So how do pardons and commutations differ? For that matter, how do they differ from clemency and amnesty?

In December 2000, Clinton granted clemency to sixty-two people—clemency being the blanket term for official forgiveness of a violation. Three of those people received commutations of their sentences—that is, they were released from prison, where they were currently serving time. The rest received pardons, or forgiveness of their crimes after their sentence was served. Pardons come in two forms: full or conditional. A full pardon is a formal forgiveness by the government that restores certain liberties, such as the right to vote or own firearms. It does not imply innocence, nor does it expunge a criminal record; nor can any fines that were imposed in sentencing be recouped. But it does make those pardoned feel better about themselves. A conditional pardon has some strings attached, such as serving a lesser punishment.

A pardon can be granted in anticipation of conviction of any crimes, as in Gerald Ford's 1974 pardon of Richard Nixon. It can also be granted posthumously. In 1999 Clinton pardoned Henry Flipper, who died in 1940, a former slave who was the first black West Point graduate and who was dishonorably discharged for racial reasons. An amnesty is an official forgetting (the word has the same root as *amnesia*) of actions against the state by a class of people. An amnesty can come with certain requirements. For example, Ford made amnesty available to men who refused to serve in Vietnam, but required community service. But in 1977 Jimmy Carter proclaimed a blanket amnesty for them.

AGENT. MANAGER.

In 1998, Mike Ovitz announced plans to return to Hollywood as a talent manager. This was thought to be a big deal, since Ovitz's last Hollywood job was as a talent agent. What's the difference between the two?

The difference is small and getting smaller. Traditionally, every entertainer would hire an agent. The agent identified projects and negotiated contract terms. In return, the agent pocketed 10 percent of the entertainer's earnings. A few big stars also hired managers, who collected an additional 10 to 15 percent. Managers helped with matters ranging from confirming plane reservations to developing a long-range business plan.

In recent years, more Hollywood stars have engaged a manager in addition to an agent, and the manager has assumed some of the agent's roles. For instance, it was reportedly Leo DiCaprio's manager—he didn't have an agent—who convinced James Cameron to cast his client in *Titanic*. Why are managers gaining influence? One explanation is that in the 1980s, superagents were overworked and could not give clients enough personal attention. So stars turned to their managers, who became increasingly influential—leading former superagents (like Mike Ovitz) to recast themselves as managers. The second advantage of managers is that they may work as producers. (Under California law, agents cannot produce their clients' projects. This prevents the obvious conflict of a producer, who wants to lower total costs, also finding himself in charge of negotiating his client's salary.) Many stars apparently prefer projects where they know the producer is on their side (and in their employ).

But agents aren't likely to be put out of business altogether, since California law also prohibits managers from directly negotiating contracts for clients. This means that—so long as the law remains intact—every star must have an agent *and* a manager, or must retain a lawyer to negotiate contracts. But if agents as a group become less involved in shaping stars' careers and become pure contract negotiators, it's possible that their percentages may fall as well or they'll be replaced by lawyers. And if managers-cum-producers become very powerful, it's conceivable that they'll fast-talk their clients into entering bad contracts.

GENOCIDE. CRIMES AGAINST HUMANITY.

In August 2001, a United Nations war crimes tribunal convicted former Bosnian Serb General Radislav Krstic of two counts of genocide, five counts of crimes against humanity, and one count of war crimes, or "violations of the laws or customs of war." What's the legal definition of genocide? How does it differ from war crimes and crimes against humanity?

When the Security Council established the tribunal that tried Krstic (officially, the International Tribunal for the Prosecution of Persons Responsible for Serious Violations of International Humanitarian Law Committed in the Territory of the Former Yugoslavia since 1991), it statutorily defined the crimes for which the war crimes tribunal had the power to prosecute.

Genocide was defined as committing any of five acts "with intent to destroy, in whole or in part, a national, ethnical, racial, or religious group." The five acts: (1) killing members of the group; (2) causing serious bodily or mental harm to members of the group; (3) deliberately inflicting conditions of life calculated to bring about the group's physical destruction; (4) imposing measures intended to prevent births within the group; (5) forcibly transferring children of the group to another group. In addition to genocide, the tribunal is authorized to punish conspiracy to commit genocide, direct and public incitement to commit genocide, attempted genocide, and complicity in genocide.

Crimes against humanity were defined as any of nine crimes directed against civilians during armed conflict: (1) murder; (2) extermination; (3) enslavement; (4) deportation; (5) imprisonment; (6) torture; (7) rape; (8) persecutions on political, racial, and religious grounds; (9) "other inhumane acts."

War crimes, or "violations of the laws or customs of war," include but aren't limited to: (1) using poisonous weapons or weapons calculated to cause unnecessary suffering; (2) wanton destruction of cities, towns, or villages, or devastation not justified by military necessity; (3) attack or bombardment of undefended towns, villages, dwellings, or buildings; (4) seizing, destroying, or willfully damaging historic monuments, works of art and science, or institutions dedicated to religion, charity, education, or the arts and sciences; (5) plunder of public or private property.

THE PERKS OF POWER

WHO CAN **LIE** TO CONGRESS?

CAN THE **PRESIDENT** CHANGE THE **OATH** OF OFFICE?

WHAT IS **EXECUTIVE PRIVILEGE?**

WHAT'S A **RECESS APPOINTMENT?**

WHEN DO **SUPREME COURT** JUSTICES RECUSE THEMSELVES?

WHAT **HEALTH BENEFITS** DO CONGRESSMEN RECEIVE?

WHO CAN LIE TO CONGRESS?

People for the American Way, a liberal advocacy group, took out a newspaper ad in January 2001 accusing John Ashcroft of misrepresenting the facts under oath during his confirmation hearing before the Senate Judiciary Committee. Is it illegal to lie to Congress?

Yes, most of the time. Witnesses in congressional hearings who make false statements under oath can be prosecuted for perjury, a criminal offense. But at the same time, witnesses in legislative hearings are covered by a common law privilege analogous to the legal privilege that protects witnesses in judicial proceedings. In this case, privilege means witnesses cannot be sued for libel or slander for the statements they make at congressional hearings. That's why Alger Hiss could not sue Whittaker Chambers for libel until Chambers accused Hiss on *Meet the Press* of being a Communist. Chambers's statements before the House Un-American Activities Committee were privileged and therefore protected from lawsuits. (Hiss lost the libel case.)

No one's suggested that Ashcroft perjured himself, only that he gave artful, Clintonesque responses to questions about his record. But what about then Senator Ashcroft's statement, made on the Senate floor the year before, that Missouri Supreme Court Judge Ronnie White had a "tremendous bent toward criminal activity"? Could White have sued Ashcroft for that?

No. Members of Congress are given an absolute privilege to lie with impunity in the House or Senate, if they so desire, by the Speech or Debate Clause in Article I, Section 6 of the U.S. Constitution. It states that, with regard to senators and representatives, "for Speech or Debate in either House, they shall not be questioned in any other Place." The Framers of the Constitution wanted to encourage debate in Congress, and they did not want that debate chilled by the threat of lawsuits. Even if White could prove that Ashcroft's statement was false, the Constitution forbids him from bringing suit.

Statements that senators and representatives make outside of the House or Senate are not privileged, however. If a member of Congress maligns you in a press release or on a talk show, you can sue him or her for libel or slander. Of course, that doesn't mean you'll win.

CAN THE PRESIDENT CHANGE THE OATH OF OFFICE?

During his 2000 campaign, George W. Bush promised that if elected he would put his hand on the Bible and add to the presidential oath that he would "uphold the honor and the dignity of the office." Can a president revise the oath of office?

No. It's a constitutionally mandated oath, not a wedding vow. Article II, Section 1, Clause 8 of the Constitution requires the president to say: "I do solemnly swear (or affirm) that I will faithfully execute the office of president of the United States, and will, to the best of my ability, preserve, protect and defend the Constitution of the United States." No one has ever deviated from the text. Even though Quakers object to swearing oaths, all presidents, even Quakers Richard Nixon and Herbert Hoover, have chosen the "swear" option. Since the oath requires a president only to execute the office faithfully, not be faithful to his wife, Bush's suggested addition would require a constitutional amendment.

While "So help me, God," is the familiar ending to the oath, it is not required. This was spontaneously added at the first inaugural by George Washington. Not wanting to mess with success, every subsequent president has said it. (The vice presidential oath, which is set out in the U.S. Code, does mandate the phrase.) A hand on the Bible is a custom from the British but not required, though all presidents have done it. Washington delivered a post-swearing-in inaugural address, which has also become standard except when vice presidents take over because of the death of the president.

Being sworn in at the Capitol by the chief justice is a matter of tradition, not law. Washington was sworn in in New York City, where the first Congress met. The ceremony didn't move to the Capitol until Jefferson's inaugural in 1800. During World War II, Roosevelt moved it to the White House because he felt a big celebration was inappropriate. Lyndon Johnson was sworn in by a federal judge aboard the presidential plane at Love Field in Dallas after the assassination of John F. Kennedy. And Ronald Reagan's second inauguration was moved to the Rotunda because of cold weather.

WHAT IS EXECUTIVE PRIVILEGE?

In February 2001, former president Bill Clinton waived his right to executive privilege, releasing some of his top aides to testify fully to a House committee about discussions of his last-minute pardons. What is executive privilege?

Executive privilege is the claim by the president that certain information is confidential and therefore not required to be disclosed to Congress or the courts. Although the phrase does not appear in the Constitution, the underlying principle does and was invoked by George Washington when he refused to release to Congress all documents pertaining to treaty negotiations. Eisenhower used it when he issued an order blocking a congressional subpoena of State Department personnel files during the Communist-hunting days of Senator Joseph McCarthy. Most often, executive privilege has been claimed to allow the president to get advice from aides, or negotiate with other heads of state, without fear that sensitive discussions will later be opened to scrutiny by the other branches. But it is not an absolute privilege, as Clinton, who invoked it big-time, discovered.

Although many presidents have claimed it, few have litigated it. The first was Thomas Jefferson. During Aaron Burr's treason trial, Burr said a letter written to Jefferson by a U.S. general would exonerate him. But Jefferson refused to release it, saying that the separation of powers made it inappropriate for the court to compel the president to do anything. The court said the president was not above the law, Jefferson turned over the letter, and Burr was acquitted. Richard Nixon was no more successful than Jefferson when he tried to keep from releasing his White House tapes to special prosecutor Leon Jaworski. While the Supreme Court found strongly in favor of the principle of executive privilege, the justices concluded it didn't apply to the tapes. Since the courts don't like to let the president use this shield simply to protect himself from his own misdeeds, Clinton was no more convincing when he tried to use executive privilege to keep aides from testifying during the Monica Lewinsky scandal.

Executive privilege has come up before regarding Clinton and questionable pardons. When Clinton released members of a Puerto Rican terrorist group from jail in 1999, Representative Dan Burton requested documents from the White House concerning the pardons. Although many documents were turned over, some were held back, with the White House citing executive privilege. Although Clinton had waived executive privilege for the hearings, if he hadn't, Congress could have challenged Clinton's claim in court. And even though Clinton was no longer president, he still had standing to invoke the privilege regarding activities that occurred during his administration.

WHEN DO SUPREME COURT JUSTICES RECUSE THEMSELVES?

Chief Justice William Rehnquist wrote that he would not recuse himself from hearing matters related to the federal government's Microsoft antitrust case just because his lawyer son, James Rehnquist, was working on a separate antitrust matter for Microsoft. When do members of the Supreme Court have to recuse themselves?

The answer is: whenever they want. Reasons for disqualification are laid out in the U.S. Code (Title 28, Section 455), but the justices themselves are their own final arbiters. According to the statute, justices, judges, and magistrates should recuse themselves if they have a personal bias concerning anyone in the case or independent knowledge of the facts in dispute; if they worked on the case as a private or government lawyer; or if they or close relatives have a financial interest in the case.

Since Supreme Court justices tend to be well off, and since lawyers often marry lawyers and beget more lawyers, money and family come up the most as reasons for recusal. Justice Stephen Breyer at his confirmation said he would not hear insurance cases because of his substantial holdings in Lloyds. Justice Ruth Bader Ginsburg participated in a case before realizing her husband owned stock in some of the companies involved. Ginsburg's husband divested as the statute prescribes.

In the Microsoft matter Rehnquist concluded, "My son's personal and financial concerns will not be affected by our disposition of the Supreme Court's Microsoft matters." In general, justices are loath to recuse themselves from cases because it opens the way for a tie. When that happens, the lower court decision is affirmed by default. If the chief justice recuses himself from a case, the senior associate presides.

WHAT'S A RECESS APPOINTMENT?

In June 1999, on the final day of a congressional recess, President Clinton appointed James Hormel ambassador to Luxembourg without Senate confirmation. The move prompted Senator James Inhofe, R-Okla., to remark, "[Clinton] has shown contempt for Congress and the Constitution." Was Inhofe right?

A recess appointment is one of the executive powers enumerated in the Constitution: "The President shall have Power to fill up all

Vacancies that may happen during the Recess of the Senate, by granting Commissions which shall expire at the end of their next Session" (II, 2, 3). The provision was originally created to fill vacancies that actually occurred during a recess, but it has since morphed into an all-purpose executive tool to counter Senate intransigence. President Kennedy, for instance, appointed Thurgood Marshall to the bench during a recess because he feared opposition from southern senators. By the time Marshall's nomination came before the Senate, that resistance had been beaten back.

Presidents also use recess appointments to delay a confirmation vote until after an election, when the nominee possesses the advantage of incumbency and, ideally, faces a friendlier Congress. President Eisenhower appointed three justices during recesses: Earl Warren, William Brennan, and Potter Stewart. All three occurred immediately before an election, and all were confirmed the following spring by a new Congress. Clinton used the recess appointment relatively sparingly; his average of nine per year is far lower than Reagan's thirty and George H. W. Bush's twenty.

WHAT HEALTH BENEFITS DO CONGRESSMEN RECEIVE?

On the campaign trail in summer 2003, Democratic presidential hopeful John Kerry touted a plan to give Americans access to the same health coverage that members of Congress enjoy. One of his competitors, Howard Dean, had been pushing a similar proposal. What sort of health benefits do congressmen receive?

Members of Congress are eligible for coverage under the Federal Employees Health Benefits (FEHB) program, administered by the U.S. Office of Personnel Management. The program covers 8.3 million Americans, from humble bureaucrats to the most powerful presidential appointees. (The commander in chief is also eligible for FEHB coverage, though it's unclear whether

President Bush has opted for such insurance.) In addition, FEHB extends benefits to retirees, spouses, and unmarried dependents under the age of 22; domestic partners are not eligible.

FEHB is renowned for offering its subscribers an unparalleled range of health-care options. In Washington, D.C., for example, federal employees can choose from nineteen different plans, ranging from fee-for-service options to health maintenance organizations. Those living outside the Beltway are guaranteed at least a dozen plans to choose from. As the program's website notes, federal employees should consider themselves "fortunate to be able to choose from among many different health plans competing for your business." The government's share of FEHB contributions was fixed in the Balanced Budget Act of 1997. The rule of thumb for congressional staffers and cabinet members alike is that the government picks up 72 percent of the average premium toward the total cost of a premium—roughly on par with what a generous private-sector employer would offer. The employee pays the remainder via payroll deductions.

AWKWARD QUESTIONS

CAN THE
**NOBEL PEACE
PRIZE**
BE REVOKED?

WHY DOES THE
**KU KLUX
KLAN**
BURN CROSSES?

WHAT IS
SODOMY?

WHAT'S AN
**IRISH
TRAVELER?**

WHY GELD A
CHAMPION
RACEHORSE?

WHAT IS
DE-NAZIFICATION?

CAN THE NOBEL PEACE PRIZE BE REVOKED?

Yasser Arafat, Shimon Peres, and Yitzhak Rabin won the Nobel Peace Prize in 1994 for the signing of the Oslo peace accords the year before. Given the violence that came later, can the Nobel Committee strip Arafat—or Peres—of his prize?

No. The Nobel Committee does not allow for the revocation of any prizes and it has never happened in the award's 101-year history. The 1895 will of Alfred Nobel, which established the prize, says it should go to the person who "shall have done the most or the best work for fraternity between nations." Nowhere in his will or the Statutes of the Nobel Foundation is there a provision for the revocation of prizes.

But that hasn't stopped several groups from trying. An e-petition conceived by a group of young Jewish professionals called for the revocation of Arafat's prize. In April 2002, more than 340,000 people had reportedly signed on. Though the members of the group acknowledge the Nobel Committee's lack of a rule on revocation, they are lobbying the committee to make an exception.

The Nobel Committee has also rejected public demands to rescind prizes of controversial laureates Henry Kissinger, Le Duc Tho, and Menachem Begin. Kissinger and Le Duc Tho were jointly awarded the 1973 prize for their success in brokering the U.S.–North Vietnamese cease-fire agreement. (Le Duc Tho declined the prize, saying peace had not yet been established in South Vietnam at that time.)

In 1982, a socialist youth group in Madrid launched a petition drive calling for the revocation of Menachem Begin's 1978 prize, which he shared with former Egyptian president Anwar Sadat. The group faulted Begin for authorizing Israel's 1982 invasion of Lebanon.

WHAT IS SODOMY?

In 2003, in the case Lawrence v. Texas, *the U.S. Supreme Court struck down a Texas law that criminalized sodomy. What is sodomy?*

The exact definition varies from state to state, but sodomy has been broadly defined as a sexual crime against nature—a phrase echoed by then chief justice Warren Burger in 1986, when the Supreme Court upheld a Georgia anti-sodomy law in *Bowers v. Hardwick.* In the United States, that language dates back to a 1697 Massachusetts law that forbade "the detestable and abominable sin of buggery [anal sex] with mankind or beast, which is contrary to the very light of nature." Buggery, incidentally, was generally accepted to mean a homosexual act; in cases of bestiality, the gender mix of the participants was immaterial.

In later years, several states formally expanded the definition of sodomy to include both oral and anal sex, whether homosexual or heterosexual. The Georgia law in the *Bowers* case, for example, defined the crime as "any sexual act involving the sex organs of one person and the mouth or anus of another." (This law was overturned by the Georgia Supreme Court in 1998.) The state law questioned in *Lawrence v. Texas* contains a similar definition, although it covers only same-sex contact. Texas was one of four states where the sodomy ban applies exclusively to homosexuals.

Broadly written anti-sodomy statutes have also been used, on rare occasion, to prosecute men or women deemed sexual deviates. Mutual masturbation, for example, was known to land the occasional couple in legal hot water, at least before the majority of states began jettisoning their sodomy laws in the 1970s. It is highly unlikely, however, that any state would pursue consenting adults for such behavior today.

WHY DOES THE KU KLUX KLAN BURN CROSSES?

In Virginia v. Black, *the Supreme Court struck down a Virginia law that prohibited cross-burning. The Ku Klux Klan, the organization most closely associated with burning crosses, identifies itself as Christian. Why do they incinerate their faith's most sacred symbol?*

The practice dates back to Europe in the Middle Ages, a period the Klan idealizes as morally pure and racially homogeneous. In the days before floodlights, Scottish clans set hillside crosses ablaze to symbolize defiance against military rivals or to rally troops when a battle was imminent. Though the original Klan, founded in 1866, patterned many of its rituals after those of Scottish fraternal orders, cross-burning was not part of its initial repertoire of terror.

Nevertheless, Thomas Dixon included a pivotal cross-burning scene in his 1905 novel *The Clansman;* he was attempting to legitimize the Klan's supposed connections to the Scottish clans. A decade later, D. W. Griffith brought *The Clansman* to the silver screen, eventually renaming it *The Birth of a Nation.* Exhilarated by Griffith's sympathetic portrayal, Klansmen started burning crosses soon afterward to intimidate minorities, Catholics, and anyone else suspected of betraying the order's ideals. The first reported burning took place in Georgia on Thanksgiving eve, 1915. Burnings have been associated with racist violence ever since.

Modern Klan groups are careful to refer to their ritual as "cross lighting" rather than cross-burning and insist that their fires symbolize faith in Christ. The days of so-called disciplinary burnings, they add, are long since over. Still, nearly 1,700 cross-burnings have been documented since the late 1980s, many of them in the front yards of African-American families—although, in fairness, the majority have been carried out by lone racist yahoos, rather than by organized Klan groups.

WHAT'S AN IRISH TRAVELER?

Madelyne Toogood, a woman accused of savagely beating her 4-year-old daughter in an Indiana parking lot, was an Irish Traveler. What's an Irish Traveler?

Irish Travelers, also known as White Gypsies, are members of a nomadic ethnic group of uncertain origin. Scholars often speculate that they are descended from a race of pre-Celtic minstrels and that their ranks were swelled by displaced farmers during Oliver Cromwell's bloody campaigns of the mid 1600s. Travelers once roamed from town to town in horse-drawn carts, earning their keep by busking and tinsmithing; because of the latter vocation, they were nicknamed Tinkers, a word that's now considered something of a slur.

Modern Travelers in Ireland, who number around 25,000, frequently live in ad hoc trailer encampments, though some have settled in permanent housing. Though prejudice against Travelers has abated over the years, they are still widely thought of as thieves and troublemakers; according to a recent poll, 70 percent of Irish citizens wouldn't accept a Traveler as a friend. A new law that criminalizes trespassing, thus making it easier for police to shut down encampments, has been criticized by Travelers as an attempt to destroy their culture.

A few Irish Travelers emigrated to America during the potato famine of the mid–nineteenth century. Their 7,000 to 10,000 descendants still speak the secret Traveler language, a dialect alternately known as Shelta, Gammon, or Cant, which includes elements of Irish Gaelic, English, Greek, and Hebrew. They are also devout Roman Catholics who rarely marry outside the group. Their tight-knit, insular clans spend the winters in such sunny locales as White Settlement, Texas, and Murphy Village, South Carolina, then hit the road come spring. Many U.S.-based Irish Travelers, including Toogood's husband, work as itinerant roofers, pavers, and painters. Police frequently warn the elderly about home-improvement scams operated by a few Irish Travelers. Wandering contractors have been known to charge gullible customers thousands of dollars for "sealants" that are nothing more than watered-down lubricant; the con artists quickly leave town once the check is cashed.

Toogood, incidentally, pleaded guilty to felony battery and received a suspended sentence, a $500 fine, and a year of probation.

WHAT IS DE-NAZIFICATION?

U.S. plans for postwar Iraq included a program of de-Baathification for Iraqi government officials, which borrowed from the de-Nazification program established in Germany after World War II. What was de-Nazification, and how did it work?

As early as August 1944, Franklin D. Roosevelt argued in internal memos that the German people must have it driven home to them that they had participated in a lawless conspiracy during the war. When the Allied leaders decided in 1945 to try major German war criminals at Nuremberg, they also agreed to pursue a de-Nazification policy for all Germans.

Under the program, the three Western Allies (Britain, France, and the United States) required every adult citizen in their zone of occupation to complete a 131-point questionnaire detailing— under threat of punishment for any false statements—his or her entire political career during the Third Reich. Authorities then examined these forms and exonerated some Germans. The rest of the cases were sent before tribunals that classified them as a major offender, offender, lesser offender, follower, or eligible for exoneration. The punishments ranged accordingly: Germans could serve jail time, lose their property, or lose their pension rights, among other consequences. In theory, all Germans would be de-Nazified before they could find new jobs.

In practice, de-Nazification ran into a number of snags. First, the program required an enormous bureaucracy the Allies were ill equipped to manage. In the American zone of occupation alone, some 10 million Germans submitted questionnaires; reviewing each one took time, and finding German speakers to run the tribunals was tough. Efforts to facilitate the process often weakened its efficacy. The authorities proclaimed general amnesties (for, say, individuals whose sole official political affiliation was with the Hitler Youth in their teens) that left some Nazi sympathizers unpunished. And some of the Germans found to run the tribunals were reluctant to dole out harsh sentences to their countrymen, especially to those defendants who had obtained affidavits attesting to their anti-Nazi behavior. These affidavits, called *Persilschein*, or laundry certificates, were often attainable from local priests and were occasionally bought.

In addition to the logistical dilemmas, the United States ran into political tangles as it administered the program, which some felt should punish Germans and others felt should be a process that reintegrated Germans into society. As the Cold War began and the United States needed to win over its West German allies, de-Nazification was thought too alienating, and the system began to peter out by 1948. Some Germans with dubious histories were exonerated, simply because their tribunals were scheduled too late.

WHY GELD A CHAMPION RACEHORSE?

In 2003, Funny Cide won the first two legs of horse racing's Triple Crown. Had he won the third leg, the Belmont Stakes, he would have become the first gelding, or equine eunuch, to earn the trifecta. What's the point of snipping a thoroughbred's manhood, especially since a gelding has no stud value?

In most cases, gelding is used as an attitude adjuster. Testosterone makes colts behave quite badly, even violently, toward humans and fillies alike. An ungelded colt will bite, rear, kick, or whinny uncontrollably and may have to be isolated from other horses to prevent such behavior. These young male horses also often refuse to obey a trainer's commands. As human survivors of adolescence can attest, a preoccupation with sexual needs tends to diminish concentration.

A large number of racehorses, then, are gelded quite young. According to the Jockey Club, 25.8 percent of thoroughbreds who raced in North America in 2002 were geldings; that figure doesn't include less glamorous quarter horses, which are also frequently castrated. The procedure is typically done within the first year of life, before the horse can develop too many of the aggressive habits of a mature stallion. Owners are careful not to geld too early, though, as such colts may not mature physically.

An equine castrato obviously can't have a post-career job as a stud, but that's not really an issue for most horses. Only a tiny fraction of professional racehorses possess the stellar bloodlines necessary to earn stud fees. For every descendant of Alydar that brings in millions from an Arab sheik, there are scores of horses that could never even show, let alone win, at Delaware Park.

That brings up yet another advantage of gelding—longevity. Thoroughbred superstars, such as the handful that appear in Triple Crown races, retire quite young, often because they're either put out to stud or slow down markedly after the age of 4. Geldings, on the other hand, can run successfully for a few years longer—the legendary John Henry, for example, was still winning races at age 9. No one's quite sure why this is, but many trainers speculate that the castration leads to less bulky—and thus less injury-prone—musculature.

Funny Cide is an exception to the gelding rules, as he was emasculated for health reasons, not behavior modification. As a yearling, he was a cryptorchid—that is, one of his testicles never dropped, but rather remained lodged inside his body—and the testicular defect prevented him from walking normally. Had Funny Cide not been gelded, he likely wouldn't have had any racing career whatsoever.

Bonus Explainer: Funny Cide is lucky he wasn't born half a century ago, or his Triple Crown dream might have been squashed by gelding bias. From 1919 to 1956, horses bereft of testicles were banned from competing at the Belmont Stakes.

SAY WHAT?

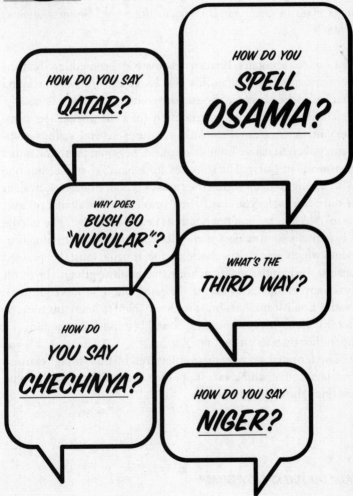

HOW DO YOU SAY _QATAR_?

The tiny Persian Gulf emirate of Qatar was vital to the U.S. military's plans in Gulf War II. What is the correct pronunciation of Qatar?

The most accurate English estimate is something halfway between _cutter_ and _gutter_. It's not "KUH-tar," the pronunciation that for a while became the standard among TV newscasters.

The Arabic language—particularly the colloquial dialect common in the Arabian Peninsula—features several sounds completely alien to native English speakers, beginning with the initial consonant in _Qatar_. The _q_ makes for a hard "k" sound, but one with its origins deep within the throat—a poor English equivalent is the _c_ in _cough_. The word's first vowel sound is similar to "aw," as in "Aw, shucks!" but not nearly as heavy on the "w." The middle _t_ is perhaps the trickiest part. It is known as a velarized consonant, which means the back of the tongue must be pressed against the mouth's roof to achieve the requisite effect. The result is somewhat similar to the "tt" in _butter_ but a lot more guttural. Native English speakers must train very hard to learn this trick, as our impulse when making a "t" sound is to push up the tongue's tip, rather than its aft section.

The terminal _ar_ is nearly overpowered by this strong velarized consonant. If anything, it is supposed to sound like a little rumble escaping the epiglottis.

HOW DO YOU SPELL _OSAMA_?

Slate says Osama. _The FBI says_ Usama. _Should we call the whole thing off?_

No! As most everyone knows, the Arabic alphabet differs from the Latin alphabet. The Arabic alphabet has twenty-eight letters rather than twenty-six, and it uses completely different characters—some of which, including the first character of bin Laden's first name, do not have directly corresponding sounds in English.

A variety of systems exist to Romanize Arabic letters and words, but there is no dominant one. The *International Journal of Middle East Studies* offers one system, the Library of Congress a slightly different one. And not all publications consistently follow one system, either. Historical tradition for a particular place or name can win out, and so can personal preference. Or the ad hoc spelling established by the Associated Press or *The New York Times* can become the standard. If an Arab attains fame in the West, academics and specialists will usually yield to the spelling popularized by journalists. For example, the *IJMES* transliteration of the al-Qaida leader would be *Usama ibn Ladin,* but the journal will probably use *Osama bin Laden* in the future. Call it the tyranny of citation.

The difficulty in Romanizing Arabic was illustrated in the 1980s by the multiple spellings for Libyan strongman Moammar/Muammar Gadaffi/Gaddafi/Gathafi/Kadafi/Kaddafi/Khadafy/Qadhafi/Qathafi. The official Library of Congress transliteration would be *Qadhdhafi,* but the library opted for *Quaddafi* instead, because the *dhdh* looked so strange in English. In 1986, most publications, including the Associated Press, adopted *Gadhafi* as the new standard. Why? The Libyan leader had sent letters to American schoolchildren and a minister under the name *Moammar El-Gadhafi.* (Before that, he had refused to Romanize his name.) The Associated Press stylebook says, "People are entitled to be known however they want to be known as long as their identities are clear."

How does Osama/Usama want his name to be spelled? In a document published by *The Wall Street Journal* on October 3, 2001, the al-Qaida leader Romanized his name as *Usama.*

WHY DOES BUSH GO "NUCULAR"?

When speaking about nuclear weapons, George W. Bush invariably pronounces the word "nucular." Is this an acceptable pronunciation?

Not really. Changing "nu-clee-ar" into "nu-cu-lar" is an example of what linguists call metathesis, which is the switching of two adjacent sounds. (Think of it this way: "nook le yer" becomes "nook ye ler.") This switching is common in English pronunciation; you might pronounce *iron* as "eye yern" rather than "eye ron." Why do people do it? One reason, offered in a usage note in the *American Heritage Dictionary,* is that the *ular* ending is extremely common in English, much more common than *lear.* Consider *particular, circular, spectacular,* and many science-related words like *molecular, ocular,* and *muscular.*

Bush isn't the only American president to lose the "nucular" war. The columnist William Safire has lamented that, besides Bush, at least three other presidents—Eisenhower, Carter, and Clinton—have mangled the word. In fact, Bush's usage is so common that it appears in at least one dictionary. The eleventh edition of *Merriam-Webster's Collegiate* includes the pronunciation, though with a note identifying it as a pronunciation "disapproved of by many." A 1961 *Merriam-Webster's Collegiate* was the first to include "nucular"; the editors received so many indignant letters that they added a usage note in the 1983 version that is still in the 2003 edition, pointing out its "widespread use among educated speakers including scientists, lawyers, professors, congressmen, U.S. cabinet members, and at least two U.S. presidents and one vice president."

These days, Merriam-Webster's sends every reader who fusses about "nucular" a defensive, 400-word response letter.

WHAT'S THE THIRD WAY?

In the late 1990s, the Third Way was all the rage. Tony Blair ped-dled the term. So did Bill Clinton. And Gerhard Schröder, the Ger-man leader, was often called a Third Way man by the press. So what is this Third Way?

In current usage, the term describes a capitalist ideology falling, roughly speaking, just left of center. But, looking back over the last sixty years, *Third Way* has been used variously and promiscu-ously enough to have lost any specific meaning.

The term has been applied to phenomena as unusual as an Israeli political party formed in 1995 to oppose Israel's withdrawal from the Golan Heights, but its broadest applications have been:

- Francisco Franco's version of fascism in 1930s Spain.
- The agendas of dissident Communists such as Marshal Tito of Yugoslavia (who broke with Stalin in 1948) and Alexander Dubček of Czechoslovakia (the architect of the liberalizing reforms in the Prague Spring of 1968).
- Mikhail Gorbachev's effort to find a route between state socialism and capitalism, including his perestroika campaign (a restructuring of the Soviet economy within a Communist frame-work) in the late 1980s.
- Movements throughout Eastern Europe before the fall of the Berlin Wall seeking more freedom under socialism.
- Socialist Sweden, straddling the divide between a centrally planned economy and pure market strategies.
- Bill Clinton's appeal to New Democrats, dating from his 1992 campaign.
- Tony Blair and his Laborites, who proclaim their split from both classical liberalism and the Thatcher-Reagan model, as well as contemporaneous movements elsewhere in Europe.

Naturally, the Third Way has its detractors. Czech president Vaclav Klaus once said, "The Third Way is the fastest route to the third world."

HOW DO YOU SAY CHECHNYA?

In television reports about the 1999 Russian bombardment of Chechnya, news anchors seemed to disagree over the pronunciation of the troubled region's name. Some stress the first syllable, while others enunciate the word with three syllables. What's the correct pronunciation of Chechnya?

The answer is "Chich-NYA," two syllables, with a strong stress on the second. But the inhabitants of Chechnya are known as "CHE-chens," emphasis on the first syllable.

Chechen is a Russian word. While most Chechens speak Russian, they also speak a distinct language called Nokhchiin, and in that tongue, Chechens refer to themselves as Nokhchi. Hence, when they attempted to break away from the Russia Federation in 1991, revolutionaries proclaimed the formation of an independent nation they called Nokhchi-Chu. And although the capital of Chechnya is widely known as Grozny (Russian for "stormy"), Chechens call it Djovkhar Ghaala. But don't worry if you have trouble wrapping your tongue around the Nokhchiin words—Westerners commonly use the Russian terms, and the Nokhchi take no offense when they are referred to as Chechens.

HOW DO YOU SAY NIGER?

In 2003, President Bush was on the defensive for erroneously asserting in his State of the Union that Saddam Hussein tried to buy uranium from an unnamed African country. The president was referring to Niger; how is the country's name pronounced?

Well, it's *not* "NYE-jur." Explainer used this pronunciation when he called Niger's embassy and was vigorously chided by the receptionist. Those in the know use the French-sounding "nee-

ZHER," and emphasize the second syllable so the word makes an approximate rhyme with *Pierre*.

Until 1960, Niger was a colony of France, and French is still Niger's official language. Its neighbor Nigeria, with which it is occasionally confused, was under English control before it gained its independence, also in 1960; that's why the pronunciations differ so sharply. What do you call someone who hails from Niger? Old-schoolers (and, in what an editor there called "something of an oversight," the *Merriam-Webster Online Dictionary*) still use the archaic *Nigerois* (nee-zher-WAH); more common and up-to-date is *Nigerien* (nee-ZHER-yen). Still, both are acceptable, as long as you don't call your friend in Niamey a Nigerian.

LAWYERING

WHAT IS A **GRAND JURY?**

CAN YOU PLEAD **GUILTY** <u>AND</u> MAINTAIN YOUR **INNOCENCE?**

CAN YOU **KILL SOMEONE TWICE?**

CAN YOU REFUSE A **PSYCH EXAM?**

WHEN CAN A **DEFENDANT** BE TRIED IN **ABSENTIA?**

DO JUDGES READ **AMICUS CURIAE** BRIEFS?

CAN YOU PLEAD GUILTY _AND_ MAINTAIN YOUR INNOCENCE?

In October 2001, former Symbionese Liberation Army member Sara Jane Olson pleaded guilty to having planted bombs under police cars twenty-five years ago and then denied her guilt to reporters moments later, telling them she entered the plea because she feared she couldn't get a fair trial in the wake of the September 11 terrorist attacks. Does a criminal or civil defendant have to believe sincerely in her plea for it to stick in a court of law?

No. In a landmark 1970 case, _North Carolina v. Alford,_ the defendant pleaded guilty to second-degree murder to avoid a trial on a first-degree murder charge—which carried a possible capital sentence. When entering his plea, the defendant claimed he was innocent of the crime but too afraid of the death penalty to risk a trial. The judge accepted Alford's plea, and the U.S. Supreme Court later held that a guilty plea made out of alleged fear or coercion is still valid: "That he would not have pleaded except for the opportunity to limit the possible penalty does not necessarily demonstrate that the plea of guilty was not the product of a free and rational choice." A 1970 California Supreme Court decision also holds that as a matter of state law, a defendant can plead guilty while still asserting innocence if there is enough evidence against her to support a finding of guilt.

While nothing required the judge in Olson's case to reopen proceedings, based on Olson's public statements of innocence, nothing prohibited him from reopening the case or rejecting her plea and forcing the case to go to trial. Judges in criminal cases are uniquely responsible for determining whether a plea entered is fair and uncoerced. Whether or not a judge is willing to accept a plea that may have been motivated by fear turns more on that judge's theory of coercion than anything else. Since up to 90 percent of criminal convictions result from plea bargaining, and at least 90 percent of the people in prison seem to insist that they are innocent, it stands to reason that the criminal justice system will not necessarily invalidate a guilty plea simply because the defendant makes out-of-court statements about his innocence. In Olson's case, the judge declined to let her withdraw the plea.

WHAT IS A GRAND JURY?

Grand juries are always in the news. But who are these people?

Grand juries make the initial decision to indict—formally accuse—a criminal defendant and require him or her to stand trial. Grand jury indictments are required for all federal felonies. About half the states have some sort of grand jury hurdle too. Grand jurors are ordinary citizens who listen to the prosecutor questioning witnesses. Unlike a trial, a grand jury proceeding is private, and there is no cross-examination or presentation of the defense case. In fact, witnesses may not even have a lawyer present during questioning. And jurors themselves may ask questions.

Grand jury service is an extraordinary burden. A typical federal grand juror serves for eighteen months, attending two all-day sessions a week, and hearing whatever cases come along. If the eighteen months runs out in the middle of a long case, the supervising judge can tack six months on to the jury's term. (After that, a new grand jury reads past transcripts and picks up where the other left off.) Occasionally, a judge will assign a sure-to-be-lengthy case to a special grand jury, which may meet for up to three years! Federal grand jurors are paid $40 per day of service, plus $3 for transportation, except for government employees, who get full pay.

Federal grand juries consist of sixteen to twenty-three jurors (it's up to the judge), but twelve yes votes are always required for an indictment. Grand jurors are selected from the same voter registration rolls used to pick ordinary federal jurors. Hundreds are summoned when a new jury is needed, and then the judge excuses people who would find it especially burdensome to give up two or three days a week for a year and a half. As a result, grand jurors are generally retirees, the unemployed, or government employees. Do we know the grand jurors' identities? Officially, no. Grand jurors can't say what case they are hearing, even after the case is over. And the court doesn't release the grand jurors' names either. However, witnesses spend hours in the same room as the grand jurors and of course learn what the jurors look like. Witnesses, unlike grand jurors, can talk about what happened in the grand jury room, and sometimes describe grand juries to the press.

CAN YOU KILL SOMEONE TWICE?

"Murder Isn't Always a Crime" claims the tagline for the movie Double Jeopardy, *in which Libby Parsons (Ashley Judd) is framed by her husband in his faked murder. Upon her release from prison, she plans to kill him—for real, this time—since, she explains, you can't be prosecuted twice for the same crime. If this plot were real, could Libby get away with it?*

Legal precedent for these circumstances is lacking. However, most legal experts agree that Libby would go back to prison for the second murder—even though the court's records would show that she was convicted of killing the victim years ago.

Libby's defense in the movie—double jeopardy—is derived from the Fifth Amendment of the Constitution, which says that no person "shall be subject for the same offense to be twice put in jeopardy of life or limb." Libby's problem is that double jeopardy can be claimed only when multiple prosecutions arise from a single criminal action. For example, a double jeopardy defense would certainly fail if a defendant claimed that he couldn't be prosecuted for a second assault on a victim just because he was convicted of assaulting her two years earlier.

The obvious objection to this analogy is that while you can clearly assault someone twice, you can kill a person only once. Therefore, the evidence that would prove Libby's guilt in one crime would necessarily clear her of the other. The problem with this defense is that the court is free to overturn or disregard earlier factual findings if new evidence—say, a recently killed body—proves them to have been incorrect. (Libby would have welcomed this flexibility if the court had discovered that her husband was alive while she was still imprisoned.) If the state (or Libby's defense lawyer) grossly mismanaged the first case in a way that resulted in her wrongful conviction, she might be able to sue for damages. But it would not affect her second trial.

If convicted in a second trial, Libby might argue that she had already served her time and should be set free. Depending on the state in which the murder was committed, the court might have some leeway in reducing Libby's sentence. But convicted murderers are almost never given suspended sentences.

CAN YOU REFUSE A PSYCH EXAM?

Accused terrorist Zacarias Moussaoui repeatedly refused to meet with his court-appointed psychiatrist. Moussaoui wanted to represent himself at trial but had to pass a psychiatric exam before the judge would allow him to do so. How can you refuse to meet with the court psychiatrist? And what happens if you continue to do so?

You can always disobey a judge. When Moussaoui refused to meet with the psychiatrist, Judge Leonie Brinkema couldn't shackle him to a table and force him to talk. We call that torture. The judge could hold him in contempt of court. But that's unlikely—and pointless. He's already behind bars.

Most likely, such obstinacy will cost you your right to represent yourself. Under the Supreme Court's decision in *Faretta v. California,* the judge must be sure the defendant's decision to fire his lawyer is made "knowingly and intelligently." Without a psychiatric evaluation, a judge may not be able to make that call—in which case she could order lawyers to stay involved.

Faretta also says a defendant can lose the right to self-representation through "serious and obstructionist" misconduct. Refusing a psych exam might qualify.

Judge Brinkema warned that she might ship Moussaoui to a federal prison specializing in psychiatric evaluation. That examination would have a different aim: to assess whether he's even fit to stand trial.

DO JUDGES READ AMICUS CURIAE BRIEFS?

A record number of amicus curiae ("friend of the court") briefs were filed in the two cases challenging the University of Michigan's affirmative action policy, which the Supreme Court heard in April 2003. Do the justices really pay attention to amicus briefs?

Amicus briefs do matter, though they rarely, if ever, make or break a case. They're most effective when they succinctly point out potential long-term consequences that the court might not otherwise recognize. In the Michigan cases *Gratz v. Bollinger* and *Grutter v. Bollinger,* for example, one of the 100-plus amicus briefs was filed on behalf of a group of former military leaders, including Norman Schwarzkopf. The brief argued that a decision for the plaintiffs would hamper the military's efforts to build a diverse officer corps, since so many career soldiers come from campus ROTC programs. And dozens of Fortune 500 companies weighed in with their two cents, contending that affirmative action abets workplace diversity, which in turn makes the private sector more competitive in global markets. (More than three-quarters of the amicus briefs in the Michigan cases supported the university's case.)

The justices may not read each and every amicus brief in its entirety, but their clerks are adept at excerpting the meat of the most relevant ones. In regard to two assisted suicide cases, Justice Stephen Breyer later remarked that amicus briefs from medical groups "play[ed] an important role in educating judges on potentially relevant technical matters, helping to make us, not experts, but educated laypersons, and thereby helping to improve the quality of our decisions." And in the famous *Bakke* case of 1978, which struck down racial quotas but left the door open for affirmative action, Justice Lewis Powell cited the quota-free Harvard plan as a model for attaining on-campus diversity; it's believed that he learned of this admissions plan by reading Harvard's amicus brief.

On rare occasions, the court may actually request that a third-party expert file an amicus brief. More often than not, however, filings are unsolicited. According to Rule 37 of the Rules of the Supreme Court of the United States, an amicus brief is supposed to bring "to the attention of the Court relevant matter not already brought to its attention by the [involved] parties." In order to file such a brief, an interested third party must first try to obtain written consent from both the petitioner and the respondent in the case. If one or the other side objects, the third party can ask the court for a motion of leave to clear the way. Over 80 percent of such motions are granted.

These days, amicus briefs are being filed more and more often. According to a 2000 *University of Pennsylvania Law Review* study, the number of amicus briefs filed annually to the Supreme Court has increased 800 percent since the mid 1940s. Eighty-five percent of the court's cases now invite such briefs, as opposed to a mere 10 percent in the early to mid 1900s.

WHEN CAN A DEFENDANT BE TRIED IN ABSENTIA?

Cosmetics heir Andrew Luster, who skipped out on a rape trial in January 2003, was later captured in Puerto Vallarta, Mexico. He had been convicted in absentia and sentenced to 124 years in prison. Under what circumstances can a person be tried in absentia?

The typical scenario involves a defendant who flees midtrial, fully aware that he or she is supposed to show up in court each and every day. Rule 43 of the Federal Rules of Criminal Procedure clearly states that a defendant waives the right to be present if he's "voluntarily absent after the trial has commenced." (Most state rules on trials in absentia are similarly worded.) A bail jumper like Luster, who forfeited his $1 million bond by walking out of a California courthouse during a recess, certainly fits into that category.

Trials in absentia are exceedingly rare—most judges and attorneys will never be involved with one. The procedure doesn't jibe with the notion of due process, especially the constitutional right of the accused to confront witnesses. So judges are careful to make sure that a defendant's absence is truly voluntary, rather than the result of foul play, ill health, or lack of notice, lest they create grounds for an appeal.

If a defendant takes off during the pretrial phase, however, he may be able to elude an in absentia conviction. In the 1993 case *Crosby v. United States,* the Supreme Court ruled that federal law "prohibits the trial in absentia of a defendant who is not present at the beginning of trial." This despite the fact that Crosby, accused of mail fraud in Minnesota, appeared before a federal magistrate to enter a plea of not guilty before escaping to Florida. As for a fugitive who has never been in custody, such as Osama bin Laden, odds are slim to none that any U.S. court would permit his trial in absentia, regardless of the strength of the evidence.

Nor can globe-trotting criminals be tried in absentia by the International Criminal Court (ICC). Article 63 of the Rome Statute, which governs the ICC's operation, simply states, "The accused shall be present during the trial." Of course, it's doubtful that anyone high-profile enough to merit the ICC's attention would be afforded the chance to skip out on bail.

DINING OUT

HOW DO **TRANS AND** *SATURATED FATS* **DIFFER?**

HOW MUCH OF THE **FOOD WE EAT** *IS* **BIOENGINEERED?**

WHY IS **CANNED TUNA** *SO CHEAP?*

WHAT IS **OVALTINE,** PLEASE?

WHAT DO THE **BRITS** MEAN BY **HORLICKS?**

CAN YOU **LIVE** OFF LIZARD MEAT?

HOW DO TRANS AND SATURATED FATS DIFFER?

In July 2003, the Food and Drug Administration announced that by 2006 all nutrition labels—which currently list both total fat and saturated fat—must also detail the amount of trans fatty acids any serving contains. But as recently as 1999, the agency was considering lumping trans and saturated fats together, listing both on the "Sat. Fat" line. How different are the two fats, and is one worse than the other?

The distinction lies in the number of hydrogen atoms each fat molecule contains. All fat molecules consist primarily of strings of carbon atoms to which hydrogen atoms can link; in a saturated fat, every carbon in the chain has as much hydrogen attached to it as possible (the fat is saturated because no more hydrogen will fit). Unsaturated fats have less hydrogen; trans fats fall somewhere in the middle and are created when unsaturated fats undergo partial hydrogenation, a process that adds some hydrogen without fully saturating the fat. (The procedure also bends fat molecules into the strange shapes, called trans configurations, that give the fats their name.)

Partially hydrogenated and saturated fats have longer shelf lives than their unsaturated peers. That's because the extra hydrogen raises the fats' melting points, making them more stable at room temperature. Trans fats are useful because they're slightly softer than saturated fats (think margarine vs. butter). And food producers (well aware that they'd have to list any saturated fats on the label) also sometimes opt to use trans fats instead so their products appear more healthful.

Now that the loophole has been closed, snackers will know what they're eating, although nutritionists are still debating whether saturated or trans fat is worse for you. Saturated fats—which you'll find in steak, ice cream, and butter—have been studied for decades, while trans fats—present in doughnuts, fries, and margarine—have been under scrutiny for only the last ten years. Both have been proven to increase low-density lipoprotein, your "bad" cholesterol indicator. LDL transports cholesterol—a waxy substance that helps rebuild cell membranes and create hormones, among other things—from the liver to the rest of the body, where it can accumulate in arteries and cause heart disease. One thing that helps keep LDL in check is the "good" cholesterol indicator, high-density lipoprotein, which carries cholesterol back to the liver. This is where saturated fat starts looking better: It increases cholesterol indicators across the board, so HDL levels rise as well. Trans fat, however, raises LDL while reducing HDL levels, and this dangerous double whammy has set nutritionists on alert.

Trans fats may also be guilty of numerous secondary sins: There are some indications that they could increase your risk for cancer and diabetes and even cause pregnancy complications. That's why the FDA will not put a recommended daily allowance next to the new trans statistic: Any amount of this stuff is bad for you.

HOW MUCH OF THE FOOD WE EAT IS BIOENGINEERED?

In a May 2003 speech at the Coast Guard Academy, President Bush blasted the European Union for restricting the import of genetically modified foods. How much of the food produced and consumed in the United States qualifies as bioengineered?

A lot more than you probably realize. Two of the nation's biggest crops, soybeans and corn, are subject to frequent genetic tinkering, often intended to help them fend off insects. Corn is commonly modified with the addition of a gene from the bacterium *Bacillus thuringiensis;* the resulting plant kills maize-devouring caterpillars. Other added genes bestow resistance to certain herbicides that might otherwise decimate the crop.

Approximately 76 percent of 2002's American soybean crop

was genetically modified (GM), as well as 32 percent of corn. (Some estimates place the corn figure closer to 50 percent.) As habitual label readers know, soybean and corn products are ubiquitous on grocery store shelves, present in everything from Pop-Tarts to veggie burgers to Campbell's tomato soup (which lists high fructose corn syrup as a primary ingredient). No government body keeps precise statistics, but a popular guesstimate among university researchers is that around 70 percent of processed foods contain GM ingredients. Considering that about 90 cents of every dollar spent at the supermarket goes toward processed foods, chances are you've been unwittingly consuming GM victuals since the mid 1990s, when they began appearing in stores.

The other two crops that are regularly modified are canola and papayas. About half of the canola consumed in the United States is GM, though the bulk of it comes from Canada. And upward of 90 percent of Hawaiian papayas are tweaked to ward off insect infestations. GM potatoes were phased out three years ago, due to consumer backlash; the fry-eating public was worried about the long-term health risks (the FDA does not review individual GM products for safety), and the middlemen who sell to McDonald's and Burger King refused to peddle fine-tuned taters. The Flavr Savr tomato, one of the first GM vegetables, is also out of circulation, but only because it didn't taste very good.

There are few guidelines regarding the labeling of GM foods in the United States. The Food and Drug Administration mandates that bioengineered foods be labeled as such only if the nutritive content has been substantially changed or if a potential allergen (like a peanut gene) has been added.

WHY IS CANNED TUNA SO CHEAP?

A May 2003 study warned that overfishing has shrunk marlin, swordfish, and tuna populations by 90 percent since 1950. Given the crisis, why does a can of tuna still cost under a buck?

Because the species that end up in your tuna casserole aren't the ones being severely depleted. The Dalhousie University report focused on bluefin tuna, particularly the southern bluefin, considered a great delicacy by sashimi connoisseurs. Southern bluefin tuna can exceed 400 pounds, though the average weight per catch is closer to 20; that catch weight has declined over the years as commercial vessels glean younger and younger fish from the oceans. The species does not reach reproductive maturity until the age of 8 (bluefin may live to 40), so overfishing has seriously curtailed the replenishment of fishing stocks. (The northern bluefin tuna, which can exceed 1,000 pounds, is also in danger, though a bit less so than its tastier cousin.)

As visitors to Tokyo's Tsukiji fish market can attest, a choice southern bluefin can fetch upward of $40,000—a price that makes it an uneconomical choice for, say, Starkist Chunk Light tuna. That's why big-time canners instead prefer smaller, less flavorful species. Albacore, the so-called chicken of the sea, is what you'll get if the tin says "white meat." Also popular are skipjack and yellowfin. The former is considered the world's most widely consumed tuna species, and cans full of these species are often marked "light tuna." All of these tuna variants mature relatively quickly, with reproduction starting at the year mark for skipjack. That means the aggressive commercial harvest has had less severe consequences for these early bloomers. The casserole-grade species are also much smaller, with the average skipjack weighing in at 7 pounds. Smaller fish tend to be more numerous, since they require less nourishment to survive and reproduce.

That's not to imply that overfishing hasn't affected fish prices for normal consumers. Once considered a cheap protein source for the world's poor, much fresh fish is now too expensive for all but affluent diners. A recent study by the WorldFish Center estimated that, in a worst-case scenario, prices for tilapia, carp, and other low-grade fish could jump by 70 percent, in real terms, by 2020. On the canned front, albacore, skipjack, and yellowfin stocks are generally considered fully exploited, meaning that a marked increase in annual catches could eventually put an end to your supermarket's two-for-a-dollar deals.

WHAT IS OVALTINE, PLEASE?

In 2002, Associated British Foods paid over $270 million to purchase the Ovaltine beverage line from Novartis AG, a Swiss conglomerate. What exactly is Ovaltine?

Familiar to generations of kids as a chocolaty treat, Ovaltine was originally concocted as a nutritional supplement for those in need of more rounded diets. In the late nineteenth century, Swiss chemist Georg Wander invented a cheap process to harvest malt extract, a syrup derived from malted barley that's commonly used by beer brewers. The barley was first allowed to germinate, or sprout rootlets, in a moist environment. Wander then used a vacuum process to dehydrate this softened grain, leaving behind a thick, sweet goo. He hoped this syrup, once fortified with goodies like vitamin D and phosphorus, would someday win the world's battle against malnutrition.

It was Georg's son, Albert, who realized that pure malt extract was unlikely to tempt too many tummies, no matter how deprived they were of vitamins and minerals. In 1904, he created Ovomaltine by adding ingredients such as sugar, whey, and beet extract to his father's creation. He marketed it to Swiss consumers as an energy booster. An instant hit on ski slopes, where the nutty-tasting brew was served piping hot, Ovomaltine was exported to Britain in 1909 and redubbed Ovaltine. The more beloved cocoa-enriched version came along a few years later.

Ovaltine may not have solved the planet's nutrition woes, but it is a lot more wholesome than such sweet rivals as Yoo-Hoo and Nesquik. Four teaspoons of Ovaltine mixed with 8 ounces of skim milk provides a solid helping of vitamins A, C, D, B_1, B_2, and B_6, as well as niacin and, yes, that all-important phosphorus. Low-carb dieters beware: The fat content is zero, but malt is an Atkins diet no-no.

Though an acquired taste, Ovaltine became popular due to clever marketing campaigns in both Europe and the United States. The brand sponsored radio shows, such as Britain's *The Ovaltineys* and America's *Captain Midnight* (the latter of which gave away decoder rings to young listeners). Ovaltine was the official tipple of the 1948 Olympics and was carried up Mount Everest by Sir Edmund Hillary in 1953. Popular adult lore held that Ovaltine mixed with raw eggs gave a powerful boost to the male libido.

Noticeably showing its age, Ovaltine hasn't met its sales expectations for some years. Analysts blame the drink's current reputation as an inducer of somnolence for the elderly, many of whom likely grew up downing the stuff in the 1930s or 1940s.

WHAT DO THE BRITS MEAN BY HORLICKS?

In 2003, British foreign secretary Jack Straw disparaged his government's prewar report on Iraqi weapons of mass destruction, referring to the error-plagued document as "a complete Horlicks"—or a total mess, as we Yanks might phrase it. What are the origins of this British put-down?

Horlicks is a brand of malted food drink, similar in texture and taste to the more familiar Ovaltine. The beverage was first concocted in 1873 by James and William Horlick, English brothers who'd emigrated to Chicago. They hoped their invention would become the baby food of the future, but it proved more popular among adults—especially adults in England, where the product was eventually marketed as a sleep aid. (The brand never quite became an icon in the United States, although American explorer Richard Byrd did name an Antarctic mountain range after the drink, in appreciation for the nourishment it provided his crew.)

Horlicks did not come to mean "mess" until the early 1980s. Urban legend holds that the company itself is responsible for the slang usage: It once aired a series of TV commercials that portrayed a stressed-out woman enduring a series of mundane catastrophes. She ends the terrible day by relaxing with a hot nip of Horlicks. British etymologists, however, view this tale as little more than folklore—after all, the point of the ad is to endow Horlicks with positive connotations, not make it synonymous with chaos. A likelier scenario is that the term was first used in polite society as a substitution for the coarser sound-alike *bollocks*—literally "testicles," but also an interjection that's best translated as a cross between "bullshit" and "to hell with it." The word is also part of an old cliché, "to make a bollocks of something," which means to screw it up royally. There's also a theory that the slang refers to the beverage's fickle nature. A little too much powder or an insufficient amount of stirring, and a glass of Horlicks can become a gritty, chunk-filled disaster.

Whatever the true story, several British commentators snickered at Straw's attempt to employ the vernacular. Though considered moderately hip during the Thatcher years, "a complete Horlicks" has been out of fashion for quite some time.

CAN YOU LIVE OFF LIZARD MEAT?

Alleged serial bomber Eric Rudolph claimed to have survived his first winter on the lam primarily by eating lizards. Could a reptile-heavy diet really keep a man alive for months?

Almost certainly not, especially given the dearth of sizable lizards in the Western Carolina mountains where Rudolph reportedly hid out. The region's most abundant species are classified as skinks and include the five-lined skink. These slender critters rarely grow longer than a man's hand and can weigh as little as a tenth of an ounce. Lizard meat provides about 50 calories per ounce, putting it on par with chicken. Assuming that Rudolph needed to consume a bare minimum of 1,500 calories per day— a very generous assumption, since winter survival is particularly grueling—he'd need to dine on nearly two pounds' worth of lizards each day. That's somewhere between 100 and 300 skinks, which means he'd have to spend virtually every waking moment turning over rocks and peering into rotted logs.

It's possible that Rudolph also incorporated salamanders into his diet, as the lizardlike amphibians are plentiful in the Southeast. Still, salamanders and lizards are hard to locate and capture, especially in the dense forest that Rudolph called home; salamanders are particularly difficult to catch, as they are nocturnal. Wilderness survival experts recommend preying on frogs and snakes instead, since they're less skilled at evasive maneuvers. Rudolph would also have been well advised to focus his lizard-hunting efforts on the early morning hours, when the creatures are sluggish because they've yet to receive adequate sunlight.

As an ex-soldier, Rudolph was likely familiar with the Army's survival manual, which contains tips on worst-case-scenario cuisine. The book clearly states that reptiles should be cooked thoroughly, as the raw flesh often contains dangerous parasites. On the plus side, cold-blooded animals don't carry blood diseases. And Carolina lizards aren't poisonous, so there's no need to worry about crunching into a venomous sac.

Although lizards are rarely eaten in the West, they frequently appear on menus overseas. The animals are considered a delicacy in China's Guangdong province, for example, though the government has been cracking down on wild-animal markets to discourage new disease outbreaks in the wake of SARS. In Vietnam, some species are believed to promote male virility, and roasted lizards are enjoyed in parts of Indonesia, Thailand, and the Philippines. Americans who've sampled lizard flesh report that it tastes like chicken.

WHILE IN WASHINGTON ...

WHAT'S IN THE
NATIONAL ARCHIVES?

WHO GETS
BURIED
IN
ARLINGTON CEMETERY?

WHAT DOES
FREDDIE MAC DO?

HOW DOES
THE U.S. MINT
MAKE MONEY?

WHAT'S THE DIFFERENCE
BETWEEN THE
INTERNATIONAL MONETARY FUND
AND THE
WORLD BANK?

WHO REDESIGNS
OUR NATION'S NICKELS?

WHAT'S IN THE NATIONAL ARCHIVES?

The New York Times *reported that former Sunbeam CEO Albert Dunlap fudged his autobiography and résumé by omitting allegations of corporate fraud he faced in the 1970s. The story cited court records obtained from the National Archives as proof. Why were the court records at the National Archives?*

The National Archives and Records Administration (NARA) stores documents from all three branches of the federal government. It disposes of court documents only with a court's permission. Such permission is rarely granted. The National Archives' regional records services facility in New York City, which stores the Dunlap case records, said it didn't believe any court records under its supervision had been thrown out. The New York facility covers holdings from federal agencies and courts in New Jersey, New York, Puerto Rico, and the U.S. Virgin Islands. Its records date back to 1685.

NARA operates the National Archives at College Park, Maryland, nineteen regional records facilities, ten presidential libraries, and two presidential materials projects. It also encompasses the Office of the Federal Register, which publishes the federal government's legal and rule-making publications, and the National Historical Publications and Records Commission, which dishes out federal dollars to state and local governments and associations for the care of historical records.

The National Archives and Records Administration was established in 1934. Its most public face is the National Archives Building on Constitution Avenue in Washington, D.C., which exhibits the Charters of Freedom: the Declaration of Independence, the Constitution, and the Bill of Rights.

Less than 3 percent of federal government records are deemed significant enough to be permanently valuable. But that's still a lot of records: 21.5 million cubic feet of original textual materials (more than 4 billion pieces of paper from all three branches of government); nearly 14 million pictures and posters; more than 5 million maps, charts, and architectural drawings; nearly 300,000 reels of film; more than 200,000 sound and video recordings; and about 7,600 computer data sets.

WHO GETS BURIED IN ARLINGTON CEMETERY?

The Army refused to waive its rules for burial at Arlington National Cemetery to allow the captain of American Airlines Flight 77, one of the planes hijacked on September 11, to receive his own plot and headstone. What are the rules for determining who gets buried in Arlington National Cemetery?

To quote a *Slate* editor, the rules "read like the fine print on an insurance policy." Here's a distillation of who gets dibs:

Former members of the armed forces: The last period of active duty must have ended honorably. Dying on active duty will get you in, unless you were serving on active duty for training only. All veterans who retire after twenty years of active military service can get in. Retired reservists are eligible only after they've reached the age of 60 and drawn retired pay, and if they also served a period of active duty other than training. (The American Airlines pilot, Charles F. Burlingame, was 52 and had served for eight years in the Navy.) All winners of the Medal of Honor, Distinguished Service Cross, Distinguished Service Medal, Silver Star, or Purple Heart get in. Any former prisoner of war who died on or after November 30, 1993, is eligible, if they served honorably in active service while a POW. Finally, former armed forces members can be buried in the same grave with a close relative who is the primary eligible person, if "certain conditions are met."

Politicians and other government officials: The president or any former president is eligible. So is anyone who held an elective office of the U.S. government, as long as they served on active duty in the armed forces. The same goes for current and former Supreme Court justices, U.S. trade representatives, Office of Management and Budget directors, Social Security commissioners, National Drug Control Policy directors, U.S. attorneys general, and secretaries of state, treasury, defense, interior, agriculture, commerce, labor, health and human services, transportation, energy, education, and veterans affairs. If they served on active duty in the armed forces, they're eligible. So are former active duty armed forces members who held a select list of offices (including the CIA director; the secretaries of the Army, Air Force, and Navy; the chairman of the council of economic advisors; the chairman of the Federal Reserve; and a variety of deputy secretaries). The final category of government officials who are eligible—if they served on active duty in the armed forces—are the chiefs of the U.S. missions to NATO, the Organization of American States, the United Nations, and a handful of specific countries, including the United Kingdom, France, Germany, Brazil, Russia, China, Mexico, Canada, Japan, Saudi Arabia, and South Africa.

Spouses and family: The spouse, widow or widower, minor child, or permanently dependent child, as well as certain unmarried adult children of any eligible veterans are in, as are the surviving spouse, minor child, or permanently dependent child of any other person already buried in Arlington. Also eligible are the widows and widowers of armed forces members who were lost or buried at sea or officially determined to be missing in action. So is the widow or widower of an armed forces member interred in an overseas U.S. military cemetery maintained by the American Battle Monuments Commission, or the widow or widower of an armed forces member who is interred in Arlington as part of a group burial. The parent of a minor child or permanently dependent child buried in Arlington based on the eligibility of another parent is eligible. However, divorced spouses, or widowed and remarried spouses, are not eligible.

WHAT DOES FREDDIE MAC DO?

In June 2003, federal prosecutors investigated the Federal Home Loan Mortgage Corporation (FHLMC), better known as Freddie Mac, for alleged deceptive accounting. What does Freddie Mac do, exactly?

Freddie Mac plays a vital, albeit esoteric, role in the American home-buying process. The company is a key player in the secondary mortgage market, which means it purchases mortgages from banks. Freddie Mac then bundles together several thousand such mortgages into a tradable security and sells the package to an institutional investor. Say you just obtained a $200,000 mortgage with a fixed rate of 5 percent. There's about a one in six chance that your bank will turn around and sell that mortgage to Freddie Mac, which in turn will package it with thousands of other mortgages with similar rates. That collection, which may be valued at $500 million or more, is converted into a bondlike security and sold to large investors who prefer relatively safe, steady assets. (Freddie Mac securities are popular among European and Asian pension funds, for example.) The return on the security may be only 4.75 percent; the other quarter point makes for Freddie Mac's cut.

The transactions obviously enrich Freddie Mac, but the company was created by congressional mandate, and the process is intended to benefit Americans buying homes. The idea is that banks will use the money they obtain from selling mortgages to fund additional mortgages; the system has increased the nation's rate of home ownership. Also, the hope is that banks will feel more comfortable offering mortgages for homes in low-income areas, since they know they can turn right around and sell the mortgage to Freddie Mac. (Freddie Mac does not purchase mortgages over $322,700 in value.)

Despite its bureaucratic-sounding acronym, Freddie Mac is not technically a government agency. Rather, it's a government-sponsored enterprise (GSE), founded at Congress's request but publicly owned by shareholders. Freddie Mac was chartered in

1970 to provide competition for the Federal National Mortgage Association (FNMA), or Fannie Mae, another GSE, which was formed in 1938 to mitigate the effects of the Great Depression (though not privatized until thirty years later). The companies are virtually indistinguishable to the layman, as they both purchase and secure mortgages for the statutory purpose of increasing home ownership.

The two companies benefit substantially from their GSE status. They do not pay state or local taxes, nor are they required to submit filings to the Securities and Exchange Commission. They also enjoy $2.25 billion lines of credit with the Treasury Department, which boosts investor confidence in the safety of their securities. The perks often attract the ire of fiscal conservatives, who characterize Freddie and Fannie as government-created monopolies.

Bonus Explainer: As for the homespun nicknames, FNMA got its moniker because of its acronym; when you try to pronounce it as a word, it comes out sounding something like Fannie Mae. When it came time to nickname the competitor, however, FHLMC didn't naturally sound like a recognizable name. *Freddie,* then, is a take on federal, and *Mac* a reference to the terminal MC.

HOW DOES THE U.S. MINT MAKE MONEY?

The U.S. Mint is releasing commemorative quarters that feature designs from each of the fifty states. The venture, which will span ten years, is anticipated to be highly profitable for the mint. How does the U.S. Mint make money?

In 1997, Congress passed the Commemorative Coin Program Act, which mandated that each of the fifty states be honored with a new quarter. The coins, with George Washington on the front and a state design on the back, are being released every ten weeks in the order that the states ratified the Constitution. (You can find a schedule at www.usmint.gov.) In passing the law, Congress cited the coins' educational value, saying the new quarters would "promote the diffusion of knowledge among the youth of the United States about the individual states." Collectors also lobbied for the change, since U.S. coin design had changed little in fifty years. But the major advantage was the potential profit.

The U.S. Mint is in a good business: It can cut and stamp a piece of metal and sell it for the face value of the coin. A quarter, for example, costs the mint four cents to make, but sells for 25 cents—an 84 percent profit margin. After paying for the mint's operations, the remaining profits go into the government's general fund and are budgeted by Congress just like tax revenue. (Old coins can also be exchanged for new ones, but this accounts for only a small portion of the coins manufactured each year.)

Although Economics 101 teaches us that the Federal Reserve Bank uses the money supply as a tool to stimulate the economy and control inflation, this does not mean that the Fed regulates the supply of bills and coins. New coins and bills are an insignificant percentage of the total money supply, which—depending on the definition—also includes checking and savings accounts, money market holdings, mutual funds, and other financial instruments. (Instead, the Fed buys and sells securities, changes interest rates, and adjusts the required reserve ratio—the amount of hard money banks are required to have on hand—to carry out monetary policies.) So coins (and bills) are simply supplied as demanded in the marketplace.

Before the state quarters program began, the mint produced between 1 and 1.5 billion quarters in a typical year. In 2000, with collectors scooping up state quarters by the handful, it made about 6.2 billion, a fourfold increase. The mint estimates that in the first two and half years of the program, it bagged nearly $3 billion in revenue off quarters alone.

WHO REDESIGNS OUR NATION'S NICKELS?

Redesigned nickels, the first since 1938, will soon be jingling in American pockets. The coins' tails sides will commemorate the bicentennials of either the Louisiana Purchase or Lewis and Clark's westward expedition. Picking the appropriate artwork is largely the responsibility of the Citizens Coinage Advisory Committee (CCAC). How can citizens join this numismatic powerhouse?

Despite the egalitarian name, the CCAC is a fairly exclusive club. The committee was created in April 2003 by a congressional act; the same law abolishes the CCAC's predecessor, the Citizens Commemorative Coin Advisory Committee (CCCAC), which had been in existence since 1993. The new group is, unsurprisingly, charged with advising the secretary of the treasury "on the selection of themes and designs for coins."

The key difference between the CCAC and its predecessor is that the upstart added two additional members for a total of nine. The first five members, appointed by Treasury Secretary John Snow, are a highly specialized lot. The law stipulates that the bunch must include a nationally or internationally recognized curator of a coin collection, an experienced numismatist, a scholar of medallic arts or sculpture, and an American historian. There's also room for one lucky bloke to represent the interests of the general public. (The CCCAC allowed for three such nonspecialist members.) Yet this is not necessarily a *Mr. Smith Goes to Washington* opportunity; it will likely be reserved for Beltway big shots. The last CCCAC "general public" appointee, for example, was Constance B. Harriman, once a high-ranking official in the Department of the Interior under George H. W. Bush. The four remaining slots were recommended by the four most powerful congressional leaders: the speaker of the House, the House minority leader, the Senate majority leader, and the Senate minority leader. Congress played no role in the recommendation of members for the CCCAC.

No one should join the CCAC for a quick payday—per tradition, members aren't paid, though their travel is comped when they attend two annual meetings.

Bonus Explainer: The new nickels will be minted for only a few years. Virginia lawmakers were upset that the changes would be permanent and thus bump off state icon Monticello from the tails side. The act thus represents a compromise, whereby the commemorative designs will last through 2006. After that, it's back to Thomas Jefferson's fabled mansion.

WHAT'S THE DIFFERENCE BETWEEN THE INTERNATIONAL MONETARY FUND AND THE WORLD BANK?

The International Monetary Fund (IMF) and the World Bank both have headquarters in Washington, D.C. What's the difference?

The job of the IMF is to protect international trade. The World Bank's is to promote economic development. Both institutions were created at an international conference held at Bretton Woods, New Hampshire, in June 1944. Both are controlled and financed by member nations (about 180 of them), with larger nations coughing up more money and having a greater say in decision-making.

The IMF's primary responsibility is preventing or minimizing international trade crises. When a country buys more goods abroad than it sells abroad, it must borrow foreign currency to cover the difference. (This is the trade deficit. It is different from the national debt, which is when a government spends more than it raises through taxes.)

Many nations, including the United States, run trade deficits and it's not a crisis. Investors are willing to loan money to healthy countries because they are confident they'll eventually be paid back. It's only a crisis when international investors lose faith and stop lending money. The nation needs the money to repay its loans and to pay for imported goods. It reneges on its loan payments and slashes its imports. The disease spreads as banks go under, other countries lose export business, they renege, and so forth. This is the disaster scenario the IMF is supposed to prevent.

The IMF has a pool of almost $200 billion, which it may lend to debtor nations at slightly below market rates. The IMF conditions a loan on reforms intended to enable the debtor to pay off its debts, which means earning more foreign currency than it spends, which means turning the trade deficit into a surplus. In other words, the price of a rescue from the IMF is to stop getting more from the rest of the world than you give, and to start giving more than you get. That is why the IMF is often unpopular.

The World Bank's job is to help less-developed countries become less less-developed. The bank also has a pool of around $200 billion, which it lends to countries. But World Bank loans are for development projects, not for trade stabilization. The idea is that they will be able to pay off the loans by making themselves more economically productive. The countries use the money to build roads, schools, clinics, irrigation systems, and so on. That is why the World Bank is generally popular.

John Maynard Keynes, the intellectual architect of the system, thought the fund should be called a bank and the bank should be called a fund.

GOING ABROAD

DOES THE **PRESIDENT** NEED A PASSPORT?

WHY DO **AMERICANS** LIVING ABROAD GET TAX BREAKS?

CAN **AMERICANS** TRAVEL TO CUBA?

CAN ANYONE **NEGOTIATE** WITH FOREIGN LEADERS?

WHAT HAPPENS WHEN A **FOREIGNER'S VISA** EXPIRES?

WHO MUST REGISTER AS A **FOREIGN AGENT?**

DOES THE PRESIDENT NEED A PASSPORT?

When George W. Bush leaves the country, does he have to take a passport with him just like every other American who goes abroad?

Yes, he needs a passport, but no, it's not like everyone else's. The president of the United States, his immediate family, certain top officials, and diplomatic personnel are issued diplomatic passports, which have a black cover and for which the bearer doesn't have to pay a passport fee. When the president travels, a team of people, usually from the State Department, coordinate the paperwork of the trip and hold on to the president's passport. After the president emerges from Air Force One, waves to the crowd, and gets in his limo, he doesn't then stand in line at customs. The State Department employees take his passport and those of the others in his entourage through the host country's customs procedures.

The United States issues three types of passports. There are currently about 52 million holders of the familiar blue tourist passport. About 450,000 have a maroon-covered official passport. These are issued to people not in the diplomatic corps who are going abroad in the service of the U.S. government—a large percentage of holders of official passports are active-duty military and their families. About 85,000 Americans have diplomatic passports. One perk of the presidency is that even when you're out of office, you get to keep your diplomatic passport. That means Bush, who had one once before, when he was the son of the president, will never have to be without one.

Bonus Explainer: If the Queen of England should decide to hit the diplomatic circuit, she doesn't have to carry a passport. The royal family's website explains that "as a British Passport is issued in the name of Her Majesty, it is unnecessary for The Queen to possess one."

CAN AMERICANS TRAVEL TO CUBA?

Former president Jimmy Carter visited Cuba in May 2002. Aren't Americans banned from traveling to Cuba?

Under the 1963 Cuban Assets Control Regulations, you're not technically banned from traveling to Cuba, but you can't spend money there, which makes a trip almost impossible. There are, however, three ways for Americans to legally visit Cuba:

1. If you're a full-time journalist, a government official, a member of an international organization, or an athlete, or are visiting relatives or doing academic research, you may visit the island at any time.

2. If your trip is fully hosted, meaning all your Cuba-related expenses are covered by a foreign citizen or organization that you don't reimburse, you're also home free.

3. If you're planning to travel with an educational or religious institution or for humanitarian projects or freelance journalism, you can apply to the Department of the Treasury's Office of Foreign Assets Control (OFAC) for a license, a process that generally takes several months. According to the Carter Center, that's what the former president's delegation did. But if you're just interested in taking some sun, don't waste your time: OFAC does not give licenses for pleasure travel.

If you're caught visiting Cuba illegally, OFAC can fine you $7,500 for a single trip, and up to $10,000 for any additional trip.

Bonus Explainer: Are the Cuban travel restrictions constitutional? In 1984, the Supreme Court ruled by a narrow margin in *Regan v. Wald* that the travel restrictions were authorized in light of Cold War national security concerns. The court hasn't considered the restrictions since the end of the Cold War, and it might rule differently now.

WHY DO AMERICANS LIVING ABROAD GET TAX BREAKS?

In May 2003, Senate Republicans looked to kill an IRS provision that allows Americans working abroad to exempt $80,000 in income from their federal taxes. Why do expats get such a sweetheart deal in the first place?

It's a carrot for those who might otherwise blanch at the idea of working in far-flung lands. The current Foreign Earned Income Exclusion statute has been part of the tax code since 1954, when it was introduced to help American businesses in their efforts to expand overseas. (The amount of the exemption has changed over the years, peaking at $95,000 in the early 1990s.) In another perk, the cost of housing can usually be excluded, too, a real boon to those living in employer-provided apartments. A U.S. citizen or resident alien is eligible for the exclusion if his tax home is located abroad, and he is either judged by the IRS to be a bona fide resident of another country or can show that he spent 330 days there over a consecutive twelve-month period.

The law doesn't necessarily benefit bankers, lawyers, and other jet-setters. Such white-collar types are often posted to cities like Paris and London, and must pay high European tax rates. An American financier living in Britain, for example, may have to fork over upward of 40 percent to the Exchequer for the privilege of residency; because foreign income taxes are deductible, that may put his taxable U.S. income below the $80,000 threshold, negating the need to pay the IRS, but that's cold comfort.

Energy-company employees, who are often dispatched to the third world on exploration gigs, have been the law's real winners. Countries in the Middle East and Central Asia, for example, often levy little or no tax on expats, so these workers take home virtually all of their pay. Housing costs in oil-rich nations tend toward the astronomical—a safe, air-conditioned town house in Lagos can run a couple grand per month—and it's all deductible, even if ExxonMobil's picking up the tab. It's often just enough of a financial inducement to convince a native Louisianan that a few years in Azerbaijan wouldn't be so bad.

CAN ANYONE NEGOTIATE WITH FOREIGN LEADERS?

In September 2002, Representative Nick Rahall, D-W.Va., led a delegation to Iraq to meet with top officials in Saddam Hussein's government. Rahall reported back that Iraq would be very interested in allowing unconditional weapons inspections if the Bush administration would stop calling for Hussein's ouster. Is it legal for U.S. citizens to conduct freelance diplomacy?

In this case, yes. Rahall cleared his trip with the departments of State and Treasury, which gave him legal cover. But more generally, the answer is a complicated one. The only law governing freelance diplomacy is the antique Logan Act, which has gone largely unenforced for more than two hundred years. Dating back to 1799, the act is named for George Logan, a Philadelphia Quaker who traveled to France with letters from Thomas Jefferson in the hope of preventing a war with the fledgling United States. President John Adams was none too pleased by Logan's action (Jefferson, though vice president, was a rival). Neither was the Federalist-dominated Congress, which passed a law prohibiting unauthorized private citizens from communicating with foreign governments to influence disputes with the United States.

Despite all this, Logan went unpunished, and it appears that no one has since been convicted of a Logan Act violation. But sometimes the act is used for intimidation. During the 1984 presidential race, Ronald Reagan suggested that a trip Jesse Jackson had taken to Cuba could be legally actionable, citing the Logan Act as the law of the land. The act has also been brandished against Henry Ford, Joseph McCarthy, Jane Fonda, and former attorney general Ramsey Clark (for an enterprising trip to Iran). Again, no convictions.

None of which is to say that private citizens can get away with anything when visiting or interacting with foreign countries. They can't export or sell arms illegally, of course. And blabbing classified information is banned under the Espionage Act—a law, unlike the Logan Act, that people have gone to jail for violating.

WHAT HAPPENS WHEN A FOREIGNER'S VISA EXPIRES?

In January 2003, the Immigration and Naturalization Service (INS) detained more than 500 men from Pakistan, Syria, Sudan, and seventeen other nations suspected of harboring terrorists. According to The New York Times, *the majority of them are being held for violating their visas. What are the laws governing expired visas?*

Contrary to press reports, visas aren't really the issue here. A visa, which is issued by the State Department, merely entitles a person to apply for entry at the border; immigration lawyers often compare visas to the numbered tickets issued to bakery customers that determine their spots in the queue. The INS decides a visitor's status, or how long he or she will be permitted to stay in the United States, a figure usually noted in a form called an I-94. Not all visitors are given fixed times; many foreign students, for example, are allowed to stay as long as they're taking a full course load at an accredited college or university.

The detainees in question are referred to as "out of status," meaning they've run afoul of the stipulations noted in their INS documents. The INS has the right to detain anyone who has fallen out of status, though they treat each violation on a case-by-case basis. Before the 9/11 attacks, the service was lenient with many visitors who'd overstayed their welcome less than six months, provided the violator in question was taking some action to remedy the situation. In addition, out-of-status visitors with pending green-card applications were often left alone. Rocked by charges that several of the 9/11 hijackers had obtained driver's licenses despite being out of status, the INS is now cracking down on violations, especially those committed by natives of nations where terrorists ostensibly reside. (Although it should be noted that some more Westernized immigrants have suffered, too; British actor Steven Berkoff, who appeared in *Beverly Hills Cop* and *Octopussy,* was deported as part of an immigration dragnet.)

Once detained, an out-of-status visitor has a right to a bond hearing. Unless the government can prove the detainee has criminal tendencies or is a flight risk, the court is supposed to grant reasonable bail. The detainee also has the right to an attorney, though not a court-appointed one. Rather than face a deportation hearing, many out-of-status visitors agree to a "voluntary" departure, in the hopes that they can reenter the United States at some later date. If a visitor is officially deported, he or she is usually considered persona non grata in the United States for a minimum of five years.

WHO MUST REGISTER AS A FOREIGN AGENT?

Khaled Abdel-Latif Dumeisi, an Iraqi immigrant living outside Chicago, was arrested in July 2003 for having provided Saddam Hussein with intelligence on opposition figures residing in the United States. He was charged not with espionage, but rather for "acting as an unregistered agent of a foreign government." Who qualifies as a foreign agent, and why do they have to register?

The Foreign Agent Registration Act (FARA) stipulates that anyone in the United States who "acts at the order, request, or under the direction or control of a foreign principal" must make his connections known to the Department of Justice. The law was passed in 1938, in response to covert efforts by Nazi Germany to spread propaganda through American intermediaries. The most infamous of these was public relations pioneer Ivy Lee. Ostensibly employed by the German Dye Trust, Lee actually worked for the Third Reich, which was looking to burnish its image in the United States; among Lee's ideas was a campaign to portray the Nazi rearmament program as integral to "preventing for all time the return of the Communist peril." FARA was drafted to ensure that the American public would know who was really funding such flackery.

The law requires that people representing foreign principals—primarily governments, but also some opposition parties, state companies (such as tourist boards or airlines), and individuals—

register with the DOJ, make public all their related income and expenditures, and keep copious records of all activities. Any statements that the registrant publishes on behalf of her client must include a footnote stating that the author is acting as an agent of a foreign principal.

Lobbyists for a few foreign corporations, like Japan's Hitachi, are registered under FARA, but most such K Street habitués opt instead to register under the Lobbying Disclosure Act of 1995. This law allows people representing nongovernmental foreign clients to register with Congress rather than the DOJ, and its reporting requirements are considered far less stringent. Diplomats, academics, and charity workers are also exempt from FARA.

Many FARA registrants belong to white-shoe PR firms like Hill & Knowlton or Burson-Marsteller, which specialize in creating positive images inside the Beltway. For example, according to a recent FARA report, the DCI Group has the unenviable task of "improving relations between the Governments of the United States and the Union of Myanmar." (The company was paid at least $100,000 for its communications work.) Also among past FARA registrants is Bob Dole, who signed up in 1998 while advising the government of Taiwan.

Before Dumeisi's arrest, there had been only three criminal cases involving FARA violations, which now carry a maximum sentence of ten years in prison; none of the three ended in a conviction.

FEDERAL JOBS

CAN ANYONE BE **SPEAKER OF THE HOUSE?**

WHAT DOES THE **TREASURY SECRETARY** DO ALL DAY?

WHO **CERTIFIES** A RECESSION?

IS THE **DRUG CZAR** HEAD OF THE DEA?

WHY ARE **FEDERAL ELECTIONS** HELD THE FIRST **TUESDAY** IN NOVEMBER?

WHY IS THERE A HOUSE CHAPLAIN, **ANYWAY?**

CAN ANYONE BE SPEAKER OF THE HOUSE?

In 1998, ex-politicos Bill Paxon and Bob Dole were mentioned as possible candidates for speaker of the House. Neither was serving in Congress at the time. Is that allowed?

The answer is yes, though it would be a historical first.

The Constitution gives the House of Representatives the right to choose their speaker, but doesn't specify a procedure. This means every session of the House must first decide *how* to choose a speaker before it can actually choose one. Traditionally, Congress has adopted the following procedure, as proposed by Thomas Jefferson. First, the party caucuses each vote to select a candidate. Second, the entire House votes on the two nominees. Since House members vote along party lines in these elections, the majority candidate always wins. Thus the really important election is the nomination vote within the majority caucus. And House rules do not require that a nominee be a member of Congress.

Bonus Explainer: Why is the outgoing House allowed to pick the incoming House's leaders? Explainer cannot think of a single good reason. One can't argue that the procedure saves the new House much time, since the nomination voting takes only a single day. On the other hand, it's not so antidemocratic either. Though the law treats the old House and the new House as distinct entities, the two bodies are often almost identical (except in extreme cases, like 1974). Moreover, the old House can't cram a horribly unpopular candidate down the new House's throat, since the majority party can always vote for the minority party's candidate. In fact, some newspapers reported that Bob Livingston, R-La., withdrew from consideration in 1998 because some Republicans threatened to vote for the Democratic nominee for speaker.

WHAT DOES THE TREASURY SECRETARY DO ALL DAY?

CSX chairman John Snow was President Bush's pick to succeed Paul O'Neill as Treasury secretary in 2002. Other than producing a sample signature for inclusion on dollar bills, what does the Treasury secretary do, exactly?

The Treasury head is essentially the chief financial officer of the United States. Like corporate CFOs, the secretary oversees the nation's accounts, including Social Security and Medicare, and manages debt—if a creditor's looking to get paid by Uncle Sam, it's technically the secretary's responsibility to see that the checks get written. He's also the official boss of such departmental bureaus as the Bureau of Alcohol, Tobacco and Firearms, the Internal Revenue Service, and the U.S. Secret Service, as well as nominally responsible for making sure the manufacture of coins and cash goes smoothly.

Of course, most of Snow's day-to-day duties will not involve signing checks, collecting taxes, or working the money-printing machines. The Treasury secretary doubles as the president's chief economic advisor and thus assists with such important matters as preparing the federal budget and shaping fiscal policy. He is expected to serve as the public face for the administration's economic programs, which involves constant trips to Capitol Hill to get legislators on board. One of Snow's first tasks, for example, was to visit Congress and push for President Bush's tax plan.

Congressmen aren't the only folks who get the Treasury secretary's hard sell. Snow powwowed with Fortune 500 executives, foreign leaders, and banking magnates, too, as he tried to get them to go along with the Bush agenda. The job's political dimension is especially important when a crisis hits, such as the rash of corporate accounting scandals that hit in 2002. In a bid to boost investor confidence, the secretary is supposed to make the rounds and preach an optimistic message. When that message stops working, as ex-secretary Paul O'Neill found out, it's time to start polishing the résumé.

WHO CERTIFIES A RECESSION?

Who certifies a recession, and what exactly does this mean?

By general agreement, the job falls to a group of prominent econ-omists affiliated with a nonprofit research center called the National Bureau of Economic Research (NBER—pronounced "en-burr" or "the bureau"). The bureau deputizes a Business Cycle Dating Committee to identify the exact month that reces-sions begin and end.

A recession is a period when the economy contracts in size, meaning that U.S. workers produce fewer goods and services. Many economists apply the label only when the contraction lasts for six or more months. The bureau prefers a fuzzier definition:

> A recession is a period of significant decline in total out-put, income, employment, and trade, usually lasting from six months to a year, and marked by widespread contractions in many sectors of the economy.

Practically speaking, the bureau measures economic health by looking at two monthly indices: industrial production and employ-ment. Sometimes these indicators move in different directions, and it's a tough call; other indicators, like inflation-adjusted per-sonal income, may come into play. But mostly they move in the same direction, and it's just a matter of reading publicly available data. So what's to argue about? Well, the trick is that you can't certify a recession until it's been under way for a while. For instance, a recession began in July 1990, yet was not certified by NBER until April 25, 1991, nine months later. Thus, there's plenty of room for reading tea leaves.

But so what? A semantic argument among academic econo-mists seems pretty far removed from what seems truly impor-tant—the actual number of layoffs, the decreases in production, and so forth. These real economic variables, of course, are ulti-mately what matters, but the widespread use of *recession* actually can become a self-fulfilling prophecy in the way that John Maynard Keynes described.

That is, sophisticated corporations make production and employment decisions based on the same raw economic data that NBER uses to name a recession. Thus, only changes in these data—and not an NBER press release—are likely to affect their behavior. But economic decisions by small businesses and consumers are typically affected by a general sense of the economy's health that can be unrelated to specific indices. If they hear *recession,* they may choose to postpone spending, which reduces sales for other companies, who may also postpone spending or lay off employees, and so forth.

Thus, maybe it's a good thing that NBER takes so long. By the time they get around to certifying a recession, we may be on our way out of one. For example, a recession officially ended in March 1991—one month *before* NBER announced that the recession had in fact begun.

IS THE DRUG CZAR HEAD OF THE DEA?

In 2001, the Bush administration nominated John Walters to be the nation's drug czar and Representative Asa Hutchinson, R-Ark., to be head of the Drug Enforcement Administration. (Hutchinson left the post in 2003.) What's the difference between the two jobs?

The head of the Drug Enforcement Administration gets to oversee the folks with guns who bust down doors and wear cool windbreakers that say DEA. The DEA is a law enforcement division of the Department of Justice; its mandate is to investigate and arrest people who aren't obeying the nation's drug laws. The agency has 9,132 employees, of whom 4,561 are special agents, and a congressionally authorized budget of $1.44 billion for this year. The DEA was formally created as a separate agency in 1973, but its functions go back to Prohibition. It also has its own museum.

The drug czar, formally known as the director of the Office of National Drug Control Policy (ONDCP), gets to oversee the folks who write a lot of reports about how the war on drugs is going and scrutinize how other federal agencies are spending their drug-fighting money. ONDCP reports directly to the White House, has about 150 employees, and has a budget this year of about $500 million. Its mandate is to create and implement a national drug control strategy and make sure the $18 billion the federal government will dole out this year to fight drugs really fights drugs in a way that is creative, implementable, and strategic. ONDCP was created in 1988, and the first drug czar was William Bennett (who wrote with Walters and John J. DiIulio, the former head of Bush's Office of Faith-Based and Community Initiatives, a now-discredited book on juvenile criminals). Each year the drug czar is required to release a lengthy annual report on our nation's drug control strategy that can be summed up as "We can lick this if we get more money." The ONDCP does not have cool jackets or a museum.

WHY IS THERE A HOUSE CHAPLAIN, ANYWAY?

House speaker Dennis Hastert, R-Ill., ended months of controversy in March 2000 when he appointed the Reverend Daniel Coughlin of Chicago, a Catholic priest, to be House chaplain. Why isn't the position of House chaplain an unconstitutional establishment of religion under the First Amendment?

The public duty of the chaplain, who is paid $139,000 a year, is to say the opening prayer each day the House is in session. In practice, the chaplain also arranges for guest chaplains, provides counseling for members, families, and staff, and performs functions such as weddings. There have been fifty-eight House chaplains in 214 years.

In 1983, the Supreme Court upheld the practice of opening legislative sessions with a prayer offered by a paid chaplain. The

6–3 decision, *Marsh v. Chambers,* was based mostly on history and tradition. The First Congress voted to appoint and pay a chaplain for each House in the very same week they voted to approve the First Amendment. Because the Congress has always had a paid chaplain, the court reasoned, the Founders must have felt "legislative prayer" to be compatible with the Establishment Clause of the First Amendment ("Congress shall make no law respecting an establishment of religion").

The court's dissenting opinion, however, noted that legislators "do not always pass sober constitutional judgment." James Madison, the Father of the Constitution, voted for the bill authorizing payment of the first congressional chaplains but later wrote that the practice was unconstitutional. He also doubted a Catholic priest could ever hope to be appointed chaplain of the House or Senate. Hastert proved Madison wrong on one point by appointing Coughlin.

WHY ARE FEDERAL ELECTIONS HELD THE FIRST TUESDAY IN NOVEMBER?

Every year, Americans voters head to the polls on the first Tuesday in November. Why are federal elections held on that date?

They weren't always. The Constitution does not stipulate the date of national elections, just that the Electoral College electors be chosen on the same day throughout the United States. When the United States was first founded, Congress met in December and usually adjourned in March. This was largely because it was the only time farmers could be away from the land. A 1792 law established that presidential elections should be held some time in November, which gave enough time to count the votes before the new congressional session started. But the dates of local, state, and congressional elections varied from state to state and year to year. In 1845, the first Tuesday after the first Monday in November became the official presidential election date. And in 1872 the Apportionment Act added the election of members of the House. (In case you were absent from school for this: Senators were chosen by state legislature until 1913.) But why Tuesday? Many people had to travel to get to the polls, and since Sunday was a day of worship, Monday was allotted as a travel day. November 1 was out because it is a Catholic holy day of obligation, All Saints Day.

SCRIBES

WHO WRITES
UNSIGNED
EDITORIALS?

CAN YOU
SUE
A JOURNALIST
FOR FRAUD?

WHO USES
FACT-CHECKERS,
ANYWAY?

WHAT ARE
BACKGROUND
BRIEFINGS?

WHEN CAN YOU
MAKE
A REPORTER
TESTIFY?

WHO WRITES UNSIGNED EDITORIALS?

Unsigned editorials are billed as a newspaper's "official" opinions. Taken literally, this is an odd notion. It's one thing for a flesh-and-blood person like Maureen Dowd or William Safire to have an opinion, but The New York Times? *So who's writing these editorials? And why aren't they signing them?*

Each major American newspaper has, in addition to reporters and editors, a small staff of editorial writers who draft the paper's official positions. Every day, the entire editorial team convenes to discuss and debate the day's topics, and then the individual writers retire to their offices to prepare the articles. Ordinarily, the editor of the editorial page has the final say on a particular issue. Occasionally—with candidate endorsements, for instance—the publisher might participate in or even make the decision.

Reporters and editors from the newsroom are never involved in the editorial-writing process. The idea is that if reporters were writing opinion pieces, it would compromise their ability to remain (or at least appear) objective. Of course, no one seriously believes that reporters are without opinions, but in American newsrooms at least, they're not encouraged to cultivate them. (British reporters have more leeway for editorializing in news stories and British unsigned editorials are often written by the newsroom editor.) This "church-and-state" separation of news and editorial was taken to extremes at *The Wall Street Journal.* For example, the newsroom declined to report on Juanita Broaddrick's allegations of sexual assault against President Clinton. So the exuberantly right-wing editorial page sent a reporter to Arkansas and published her piece on the Broaddrick allegations. The *Journal*'s Washington bureau chief wasn't even aware of the editorial page's decision until the story appeared in his own paper.

And why aren't unsigned editorials signed? The reason is that individual editorials are supposed to reflect the collective judgment of the entire editorial board. Though written by different people, they are also supposed to speak with one voice and be philosophically consistent. In practice, of course, editorial boards don't really agree on every issue.

WHO USES FACT-CHECKERS, ANYWAY?

The scandal at The New York Times *involving Jayson Blair—the reporter fabricated or plagiarized details in various news stories— begs a question: Why didn't the Gray Lady's fact-checkers catch these slipups before they ran?*

Because, like virtually every other daily, the *Times* doesn't use fact-checkers to verify stories before publication. According to the paper's "Guidelines on Our Integrity," writers are usually solely responsible for checking such details as spellings, geographical locations, and titles. The research desk sometimes assists with more esoteric queries, and when a deadline is particularly pressing, a reporter may ask the copy desk to confirm a fact. But on the whole, the accuracy burden sits squarely on the reporter's shoulders.

No professional organization keeps statistics on the percentage of newspaper stories that are fact-checked, but the consensus is that it's quite low. The sheer volume of articles would overwhelm any research department, and there is too little time between writing and publication—often just a matter of hours. Exceptions are sometimes made for large-scale investigative pieces, which aren't as time-sensitive; they are checked primarily for legal reasons, to ward off potential libel suits. Recently, a few papers, such as the *San Jose Mercury News,* have experimented with fact-checking the most complicated science or technology stories by submitting them to expert advisors for review.

The fact-checking rules are quite different in the magazine world, where pre-publication vetting is the norm. Writers are typically asked to annotate their work, to indicate where each fact came from. In addition, a list of sources must be submitted, along with contact information and any relevant documents. Guidelines vary, but the most meticulous magazines do not allow writers to submit other articles—often obtained via databases like Nexis—as acceptable sources. Primary sources are required. Interns carry the fact-checking load at smaller publications, while the more prominent weeklies and monthlies favor professional research departments, staffed by a mix of career checkers and young, aspiring writers. Magazine checkers do not verify quotes word for word, but everything else is up for nitpicking; a magazine researcher, for example, would have asked the family of Private First Class Jessica Lynch if their home did indeed overlook "tobacco fields and cattle pastures," as Jayson Blair fibbed.

Of course, that's not to say magazine checkers are faultless. *New Republic* prevaricator Stephen Glass fooled his publication's checkers by asking that they not contact his "secret" sources, lest these imaginary informants turn skittish. On the other hand, the hoax was exposed by *Forbes Digital Tool* reporter Adam L. Penenberg, who relied heavily on the assistance of *Forbes* researcher Linda Stinson.

CAN YOU SUE A JOURNALIST FOR FRAUD?

The Associated Press alleged that forty stories written by ex-reporter Christopher Newton contain quotations from made-up sources, such as "Tim Dale" of the "Malen Clinic" and "Lynne Hallard" of "Civil Liberties Focus." Can a journalist be prosecuted for fabricating sources?

Theoretically, but it would be a precedent-setting stretch. Inventing sources is not a crime in and of itself, although it certainly violates every code of journalistic ethics known to man. A criminal fraud case would require that the reporter's deceit had been malicious and resulted in financial gain. The latter, in particular, would be difficult for a prosecutor to prove, since a published story is not intended to attract investment or gifts. Quoting "Hugh Brownstone" of the "Intergon Research Center" in his story on stealth bombers, for example, did not net Newton any additional revenue.

A duped newspaper or magazine could contend that a fiction-spouting journalist obtained part of his salary via fraud, and use a criminal proceeding to try to recoup that money. Given the profession's notoriously low wages, however, it's probably not worth the publicity headache and legal fees. No news organization has ever pursued such a case.

Civil action is a different matter. Newton could be sued for libel if any group feels misrepresented by one of his alleged fabrications. Antidrug crusaders DARE once sued *New Republic* fantabulist Stephen Glass over a critical piece he published in *Rolling Stone,* which was later found to contain several trumped-up quotes and anecdotes. DARE settled the case in 1999 in exchange for an undisclosed sum and a written apology. A companion $50 million lawsuit against *Rolling Stone* was later dismissed, on the grounds that the magazine had not acted with actual malice in publishing the article.

WHAT ARE BACKGROUND BRIEFINGS?

A February 20, 2002, USA Today story quoted "a Pentagon official, who asked that his name be withheld." Who are those anonymous officials, and how do the papers get to them?

Sometimes specific reporters cajole unnamed officials into talking, but the Pentagon often delivers them and their quotations en masse to the press at backgrounders, as it did for the *USA Today* story. The Pentagon website defines backgrounders as "news briefings or news interviews for which the spokesman is not identified by name." The State Department and White House hold similar briefings, as do the various agencies and departments, and the contents of some of them eventually make their way online.

But the Pentagon promptly posts every transcript of its anonymous briefings.

Spokesperson Lieutenant Colonel Ken McClellan explains that the Pentagon uses backgrounders when it wants an in-house expert to speak on an issue but wants to deflect attention from the identity of the speaker himself, often because the briefing is given by somebody in a sensitive position—for example, an intelligence officer. The briefers aren't supposed to tell reporters their names and are instructed to introduce themselves simply as senior defense officials (or defense officials, if they're more middle management).

But sometimes they give themselves away. Check out this snippet from a backgrounder on drones:

> **Senior Defense Official:** Good afternoon, I'm—(name and identification deleted)—for tactical UAVs.
> **Q:** Strike that.
> **Q:** (Inaudible.)
> **Senior Defense Official:** Oh. Okay. Sorry about that. (Laughter.) In any case, I am—(briefer identity deleted)—for tactical UAVs . . . (laughter).

How do the media deal with the institutionally induced anonymity? News stories often make no mention that the prized anonymous quote harvested for the story was given in front of a gaggle of reporters. For example, after a budget backgrounder, the *Chicago Tribune, The Boston Globe,* Fox News Channel, and others all cited the senior defense official without noting the context.

WHEN CAN YOU MAKE A REPORTER TESTIFY?

In June 2002, the UN war crimes tribunal ordered former Washington Post reporter Jonathan Randal to testify in the trial of Radoslav Brdjanin, a Bosnian Serb official accused of ethnic cleans-

ing. (Randal had interviewed the accused in 1993.) Would Randal have been treated any differently by an American court?

Journalists are protected in most states by shield laws, which safeguard the press from having to reveal the identity of sources or other information sought by the government. Some shield laws, including New York's, protect journalists from testifying about nonconfidential matters like an on-the-record interview—unless the information is critical for the prosecution and unavailable elsewhere. The information sought in the Randal case wasn't critical. Prosecutors were presumably building their case on evidence more damning than Randal's 1993 interview, in which Brdjanin talked about pushing non-Serbs out of Bosnia. There was also a better source for the same information: the translator on whom Randal relied to interview Brdjanin. But there was a twist to this case that probably *would* have forced Randal to testify in a New York court. According to press reports, Randal voluntarily spoke with a UN investigator and verified the accuracy of his article. Bad move. Under New York state law, by discussing the article with, say, a detective, Randal would waive his journalistic privilege. In which case he'd have to slog into court, at least to testify on the accuracy of the story.

MOVING ON

ARE **CONCESSION** SPEECHES BINDING?

HOW CAN A **COLLEGE PROFESSOR** LOSE TENURE?

CAN YOU **RECALL** YOUR GOVERNOR?

WHO GETS TO **KEEP THEIR** GOVERNMENT TITLES?

COULD **CLINTON** RETURN AND RUN FOR **VICE PRESIDENT?**

CAN THE **POPE** RETIRE?

ARE CONCESSION SPEECHES BINDING?

During the hectic close of the last presidential election, Al Gore called up George W. Bush and announced he was going to concede, and then phoned back to say he'd changed his mind. If Gore had made his concession public, would the election have ended there?

The concession speech is one final, humiliating trial for a losing presidential candidate, but it has the advantage of being non-binding. Of course, that's perhaps its only advantage. Concession speeches are ignored entirely unless they're bad, since the nation is busy giving its full attention to the president-elect. Refusing to concede, on the other hand, can make a candidate look like a sore loser.

Faced with such daunting circumstances, is it even worth conceding? Some would say no. Bush versus Gore has its closest historical parallel in 1876, when Rutherford B. Hayes and Samuel J. Tilden struggled through a closely contested election and found themselves mired in accusations of voting fraud. Hayes narrowly prevailed through his party's backroom dealing in Congress and won the electoral college by a single vote. Tilden did not concede. In fact, it was three months after Hayes's inauguration before Tilden finally spoke up, saying, "The sovereignty of our people shall be rescued from this peril and reestablished."

In 1960, Richard Nixon made a "half concession" on election night at a point when it looked like John Kennedy had pulled ahead, saying, "If the present trend continues, Senator Kennedy will be the next president of the United States." But soon the numbers began moving against Kennedy, and the exhausted Nixon went to sleep at four A.M. thinking he had a chance. After his daughter woke him to tell him the final news of his defeat, Nixon had his press secretary read a congratulatory telegram sent to Kennedy.

In Florida in 2000, where the election margin was less than

half of one percent, a recount was automatic. So even if Al Gore had conceded (and stayed conceded), the recount would still have happened. If Gore had won the recount and Bush didn't challenge it, Gore would have become president.

HOW CAN A COLLEGE PROFESSOR LOSE TENURE?

Sami Al-Arian, arrested in February 2003 on charges of abetting the Palestinian Islamic Jihad, was a tenured computer science professor at the University of South Florida. How can a faculty member be stripped of tenure?

The exact procedure varies from campus to campus, but tenured professors are generally guaranteed the right to a fair hearing before a committee of their peers. The administration must convince the committee that the professor in question is guilty of either moral turpitude (such as sexual harassment) or gross incompetence (such as repeatedly missing class). Alternately, the university can try to argue that the professor's entire department is no longer financially viable and must therefore be dismantled. Although the popular perception is that tenured professors are almost never terminated, the National Education Association contends that 2 percent of tenured faculty are dismissed each year. Several state university systems now conduct periodic post-tenure reviews to determine whether established professors are taking it a bit too easy. Tenured faculty who are terminated for cause often sue their institutions in state court, claiming due process was not followed or the evidence of misconduct was not convincing.

So why didn't Al-Arian lose his job as soon as he was accused of raising funds for Islamic extremist groups? The University of South Florida's Board of Trustees voted in December 2001 to fire the controversial professor, but USF's Faculty Senate voted overwhelmingly to retain Al-Arian. As the debate over Al-Arian's fate raged, USF adopted a new set of guidelines governing the job security of tenured faculty. Professors can now be axed for any of fourteen different reasons, including "any other properly substantiated cause or action that is detrimental to the best interests of the university, its students, or its employees." The university insisted that the adoption of the new rules, among the nation's most stringent, had nothing to do with the Al-Arian matter.

CAN YOU RECALL YOUR GOVERNOR?

California underwent a recent spasm of electoral turmoil when voters decided whether to recall Governor Gray Davis. Since the Golden State has a rep for setting national trends, should the leaders of, say, Colorado and Connecticut be worried? How many states actually allow voters to recall a governor?

While most states allow governors to be impeached, only eighteen states have voter-recall provisions. The states are Alaska, Arizona, California, Colorado, Georgia, Idaho, Kansas, Louisiana, Michigan, Minnesota, Montana, Nevada, New Jersey, North Dakota, Oregon, Rhode Island, Washington, and Wisconsin. But even if you live in one of those states, your budget deficit is spiraling out of control, and your governor can't show his face without threat of bodily injury, you still may not be jumping on California's recall bandwagon anytime soon. For one thing, although a California governor can be ousted for pretty much any reason, six of these other states require the chief executive to have committed specific wrongs. These include actual crimes and other malfeasance. For example, the governor of Alaska would be risking recall if convicted of a "crime involving moral turpitude."

When it comes to gathering petition signatures to force a recall, California also has one of the easiest thresholds to meet. It requires only 12 percent of the number of people who actually voted in the last election to sign up. Most other recall states demand at least twice that, or 25 percent. In Kansas it's 40 per-

cent. Still, even though Californians had launched thirty-one previous efforts to recall governors, none had ever made it to the ballot before. In fact, only once in American history has a governor
been shown the door in midterm by voters. That was in North
Dakota in 1921.

Recalls are much more common at the local level. According
to the National Civic League, 61 percent of American cities allow
such elections, and thousands have been successful over the
years. And although most state recall laws date to the Progressive
Era in the early twentieth century, the idea was present in America's first governing document. The Articles of Confederation
allowed states to recall their delegates to Congress at any time.
However, today's federal officeholders have to worry only about
impeachment.

WHO GETS TO KEEP THEIR GOVERNMENT TITLES?

*Secretary Albright, Secretary Cohen, Secretary Cuomo—are former
cabinet secretaries within their rights to use their old titles?*

No. Cabinet secretaries and even presidents can pack up their
embossed matchbooks when they depart from office, but they are
then supposed to leave their titles behind. That means Albright,
Cohen, and Cuomo should be referred to as Ms. and Mr. (or Dr.
if they're M.D.s or Ph.D.s).

The founding fathers thwarted the impulse toward self-inflation
when they wrote, in Article I, Section 9 of the Constitution, "No
title of nobility shall be granted by the United States." Since Americans can't run around calling themselves viscount and marquis,
it's generated a huge hunger to hang on to that high government
title. According to the State Department Office of Protocol, even
ambassadors are supposed to revert to Mr. or Ms. once they return
from Barbados. The exception is those few ambassadors given a lifetime designation of the title by the president and Senate in recognition of distinguished service. For example, Ambassador Thomas

Pickering, who served as undersecretary of state under Bill Clinton, is one.

If you want a title you can properly parade for a lifetime, become a governor or a U.S. senator. They get to keep theirs, but not members of the House of Representatives. Supreme Court justices get both lifetime tenure and lifetime titles. And once a four-star general or admiral, always a general or an admiral. If all else fails, anyone who has won elective office, held a position appointed by the president, or been confirmed by the Senate gets to be called Honorable in formal address for the rest of their days.

COULD CLINTON RETURN AND RUN FOR VICE PRESIDENT?

As Al Gore searched for a running mate in 2000, Thomas Friedman of The New York Times *facetiously suggested adding Bill Clinton to the ticket. Could a two-term president like Clinton return and run for veep?*

The answer is: He could. The Twelfth Amendment states that anybody who is eligible for the presidency under Article II of the Constitution (a natural-born citizen age 35 or older) is eligible for the vice presidency. Clinton is a natural-born citizen over 35, so he qualifies. The putative roadblock to a Clinton vice presidency—the Twenty-second Amendment—doesn't apply. This hastily worded and passed amendment, designed to block another multi-multi-term presidency such as Franklin Roosevelt's, only bars the election of a president to more than two terms in that office. It doesn't prevent a two-term president from running for the vice presidency.

The Twenty-fifth Amendment affords Clinton another route to the vice presidency: In the event the vice presidency is vacated, the president appoints a new veep, subject to confirmation by Congress. (This is how Gerald Ford and Nelson Rockefeller became vice president.) So a Democratic president could conceivably appoint Clinton. And if Clinton somehow landed in the number two spot, nothing in the Constitution would prevent him from becoming president via succession—if, say, the sitting president died in office.

Finally, another scenario could return Clinton to the White House without a pit stop at the vice presidency. If both the presidency and the vice presidency were vacated and Bill Clinton were the speaker of the House, he would become president under the 1948 presidential succession act.

CAN THE POPE RETIRE?

Since Pope John Paul II is in his eighties and ailing, can he resign and allow the College of Cardinals to choose the next pope now?

Popes can retire—the official word is *abdicate*—but the last wholly voluntary abdication took place in 1294. That was by Celestine V, a hermit who hated being pope and resigned after less than four months in office. There have been a handful of other, more controversial abdications (Was the removal forced? Was the pope legitimate?), but the last one of these was in 1415.

Just because no pope has abdicated for centuries doesn't mean that a resignation by John Paul isn't much discussed. One of the men he elevated to cardinal, Karl Lehmann of Germany, suggested in a radio interview that because of his health, John Paul might consider stepping down. But John Paul has given no indication that he wants to be around for the party to celebrate the selection of the 263rd pope. As for what happens if a pope becomes permanently incapacitated, there is currently no mechanism for removing him from office. After a pope does die and before a successor is chosen, a cardinal is designated to oversee the day-to-day administration of the Vatican, but he is not considered to have papal authority.

ACKNOWLEDGMENTS

The confines of this book prevent us from adequately thanking the writers of *Slate*'s Explainer column, who generated just about every word you see here. The four shining stars are Bruce Gottlieb, Brendan I. Koerner, Chris Suellentrop, and Emily Yoffe. Others who donned the Explainer cap and can find their work in these pages are Matt Alsdorf, Julie Bosman, Andy Bowers, Michael Brus, Michael Crowley, Ed Finn, Brandt Goldstein, Maura Kelly, Dahlia Lithwick, Chris Mooney, David Plotz, Ted Rose, Kate Taylor, June Thomas, Julia Turner, Eric Umansky, Eugene Volokh, Ben Wasserstein, and Avi Zenilman.

Double thanks go to Michael Kinsley and Jack Shafer, who gave a spit polish to many of these columns before publication; and plaudits to *Slate*'s copy staff, who make the magazine presentable every day. Finn and Zenilman stood by as ace rewrite men and fact-checkers as the book came together. Still more plaudits to *Slate*'s editor in chief, Jacob Weisberg, for his advice and support.

The book and column would be impossible without a daily assist from *Slate*'s posse of loyal readers, who send us mind-bending questions every day. For anyone harboring such a query, the door is always open: Send mail to explainer@slate.com

ABOUT THE EDITOR

Bryan Curtis is *Slate*'s associate editor. He was born in Fort Worth, Texas.